The Breaking of the English Working Class

About Salvage Editions

Salvage Editions is a collaboration between Verso Books and *Salvage*. Edited by the Salvage Collective, the series publishes writers the editors admire on various topics. Some of these interventions extend and develop arguments initially published in *Salvage*, others are entirely new. As with all *Salvage*'s publishing, Salvage Editions intervenes in the key theoretical and political questions thrown up by our moment in ways both politically incisive and stylistically ambitious and engaged. The Salvage Collective does not believe, put simply, that radical writing should not also strive for beauty.

Since 2015, *Salvage* has been publishing essays, poetry, fiction and visual art in its print edition, currently published twice a year. In 2020, along with the Salvage Editions book series, the Salvage Collective also began a live online events series in collaboration with Haymarket Books, called Salvage Live.

Over the years and issues, a cluster of concerns has emerged as core to *Salvage*'s project, including global political economy; modern political subjectivity; the social industries; sexuality, race and identity; and eco-socialism.

For more on *Salvage* and for information about subscribing, please visit the website at salvage.zone.

The Breaking of the English Working Class

Jonas Patrick Marvin

VERSO
London • New York

For Michelle and Stephen, for teaching me how to read, write, care and laugh.

First published by Verso 2026

The manufacturer's authorised representative in the EU for product safety (GPSR) is
LOGOS EUROPE, 9 rue Nicolas Poussin, 17000, La Rochelle, France
contact@logoseurope.eu

1 3 5 7 9 10 8 6 4 2

Verso
UK: 6 Meard Street, London W1F 0EG
US: 207 East 32nd Street, New York, NY 10016
versobooks.com

Verso is the imprint of New Left Books

ISBN-13: 978-1-80429-551-9
ISBN-13: 978-1-80429-553-3 (US EBK)
ISBN-13: 978-1-80429-552-6 (UK EBK)

British Library Cataloguing in Publication Data
A catalogue record for this book is available from the British Library

Library of Congress Cataloging-in-Publication Data

Names: Marvin, Jonas Patrick author
Title: The breaking of the English working class / Jonas Patrick Marvin.
Description: London ; New York : Verso Books, 2026. | Series: Salvage editions | Includes bibliographical references.
Identifiers: LCCN 2026012569 (print) | LCCN 2026012570 (ebook) | ISBN 9781804295519 paperback | ISBN 9781804295533 ebk
Subjects: LCSH: Working class – Great Britain | Social classes – Great Britain | Great Britain – Social conditions – 21st century | Great Britain – Economic conditions – 21st century
Classification: LCC HD8391 .M37 2026 (print) | LCC HD8391 (ebook) | DDC 305.5/620941 – dc23/eng/20260501
LC record available at https://lccn.loc.gov/2026012569
LC ebook record available at https://lccn.loc.gov/2026012570

Typeset in Fournier by MJ & N Gavan, Truro, Cornwall
Printed and bound by CPI Group (UK) Ltd, Croydon, CR0 4YY

Contents

Preface

Class is everywhere. The mould growing in the corner of your bedroom that your landlord refuses to do anything about is a sign of class power. Your employer scolding you for putting your jacket on too early, just a few minutes before you're due to leave work, is a demonstration of class domination. The stress, back pains and alienation you feel coursing through your body on a day-to-day basis are more often than not markers of class. The extraction of your time through monotonous work and the inability of that paid labour to facilitate you living a good life are both the products of the class society we all inhabit. Class is not experienced equally or evenly by everybody. Depending on where you live, where you work, how you are racialised, the gender you're assigned or which you choose, and much else, class can be lived differently. The Eritrean Uber driver realises class in a far more intensely violent fashion than the job coach at the Department for Work and Pensions (DWP) office. The driver is paid less, endures bodily risk to pay the rent, and is forced to limit social and family life in the process. She works under constant fear of job insecurity and, by extension, status anxiety – with her citizenship in this country perpetually under threat. Her humanity is diminished by the reality of class, and the way it intersperses with experiences of racialisation. The DWP job coach, working every day to funnel poor and vulnerable people into work, disciplining his own class brethren with sanctions, also loses his humanity as he wields power over other working-class people. Class is everywhere, but it is so often spoken about as something else entirely.

Wealthy tycoons Alan Sugar and Charlie Mullins both make a big deal out of their humble proletarian origins. But what does it mean to take someone's background, their accent or the fact that they like to don a flat cap as illustrative of their class position, when they also hire, fire, own assets, exploit and dominate other human beings daily? This isn't to deny that class can be experienced culturally, in the ways we live, make sense of the world, eat, communicate and socialise. It is, however, to state at the very outset of this book that class is often mobilised as a signifier to tell a different story, and to obfuscate the structural relations which make our lives a misery. Everybody talks about class – across the media, in politics, in the office or on the smartphone – but rarely does anyone speak incisively about the realities of inequality in today's society.

Karl Marx, the great critic of the totalising structure of oppression we call capitalism, was keenly interested in how classes are made and how they remake themselves over time. Throughout his magnum opus, *Capital: A Critique of Political Economy*, are reflections on how states and employers mould labouring populations and their dependants into subjects capable of selling their labour power to the hells of early British capitalism's socialised industrial experience. In Chapter Twenty-Five, the German social theorist's famous 'General Law of Capital Accumulation', he narrates a cycle of attracting and repelling workers to and from the labour market amid fluctuations in capital's needs, producing inequalities and stratifications among proletarians. These cycles influence how much workers earn, how much power they have and what their life prospects might be. The different moments of the cycle shape how dependent a worker is on an employer, but also the relationship of the state to workers and workers to other workers – generating divisions, forms of partisanship and cultures of recrimination between workers who find themselves competing with one another. Marx relates the cycle to the state of the population-at-large. For Marx, the health, wealth and general life conditions of the population were not intrinsically eternal and biophysical laws – they were closely tied to cycles of capital accumulation.

But the condition of possibility for capital accumulation is the fact that class is a relationship of power: between worker and employer, tenant and landlord, people and state, community and corporation. This book charts the story of how these sets of relationships have evolved, clashed, transformed and shaped the very fabric of British society today. Underlying the mismatches between class realities and images of class in contemporary Britain is a *fundamental crisis of class subjectivity*. Since I was a teenager, I have witnessed and partaken in a number of social movements and struggles that have had class at their heart. In 2010, I watched as university and college students, many of whom were working class like me, the first in their families to go to university, took to the streets and fought against the trebling of tuition fees and the scrapping of the Education Maintenance Allowance. A year later, I took part in what the late broadcaster and Black Power activist Darcus Howe described as an 'insurrection', with thousands of working-class youth letting out their anguish at the state harassment, racism and austerity symbolised in the police murder of Mark Duggan. Throughout the 2010s, I joined others in mobilising against a far right which appropriated a language of class to talk about how white people had become the victims of a Muslim and migrant minority who were taking their jobs, grooming their daughters and stealing their resources. While we were able to defend our communities from the violence of street fascism, we had less success in making the case that Muslims are disproportionately part of the working class, with far more in common with white workers than hucksters like Tommy Robinson would ever care to admit. This became clear in the late 2010s, when I witnessed, alongside millions of others, the decapitation of a project for collective working-class advancement led by Jeremy Corbyn, by the adept mobilisation of a popular zero-sum resentment, through the Brexit referendum and the subsequent 2019 general election. In the 2020s, a Black Lives Matter movement of hundreds of thousands highlighted how the lives of countless working-class people in Britain are made doubly difficult by the experience of race and class. We have seen a Palestine solidarity movement involving millions, most of whose participants are from working-class backgrounds and see in Israel's barbaric treatment of the Palestinians an image of how we are all violated and made disposable by this capitalist system. And we have witnessed a strike wave involving millions of workers from the railways and private transport (such as coach drivers), the health industry, the public sector and the postal service, keen to resist the rising cost of living.

But, despite over fifteen years of class-motivated mass mobilisations, the representations of class which have come to dominate the popular imagination are too often focused on race and geography. The spectre of the 'white working class' or the 'left behind' communicates a sense in which some working-class people are deemed to belong to the broader national and racial community of this country, while others – Muslims, migrants, refugees, the unemployed and the criminalised – are painted as unbelonging, or as threats. Similarly, we are told that class is a phenomenon that happens in some places and not others. In London, metropolitan renters have escaped issues of class by dint of their cultural capital, whereas the landlord in a postindustrial town such as Macclesfield is prolier-than-thou. This rearticulation of class around space and race is undergirded by the fact that a fighting working-class movement, capable of defending the collective interests of all who may be dependent on a wage, a benefit or a state pension to subsist, is weaker than ever. Strike rates remain historically low, trade unions are largely in decline and the idea of a universal class organising for its own interests, in the economy, in society and in politics, is hard to imagine today. Class experiences, feelings, motivations and even actions exist everywhere and emerge in sometimes spectacular moments of mobilisation, but these repeatedly fail to establish their own durable institutions of rebellion or forms of leadership. The idea of a working-class subject as a collective actor capable of regulating capitalism, or transcending it and building an emancipatory future, seems like a distant dream. This book asks how this came to be, why class dominates in the ubiquitous but shallow ways it does, and how what we witness today reflects a stasis among elites and radicals alike. Today, our rulers cannot produce the kind of subjects necessary to make a more successful capitalism, and radicals struggle to cultivate and spread the kinds of politicised agency which might upend this increasingly miserable society.

You cannot trace the history of British capitalism without a grasp of how populations have been moulded and then transformed themselves in response. A tale of the shifting sands of class domination across multiple regimes of capitalist order, this book traces the methods through which the British capitalist system, specifically in England, organises populations along class lines, mobilising forms of social oppression or aspects of social life as tools for constructing obedient and productive subjects. Predominantly concerned with how transformations in capitalist control, shape and transform the texture of economic space and the character of labour markets, this account shows that when capitalism throws human beings into different types of production, dividing them by race, gender or nation, it also produces different kinds of people. These cohorts of the population then develop novel forms of politics and cultures through which to understand, accept and resist the world around them.

Conservative class warrior Margaret Thatcher pursued a militant quest to transform the 'human soul'. This book examines how it was transformed, and into what. Following the transition from postwar social democracy and the neoliberal period of deregulated labour markets, disempowered popular classes, privatised means of social reproduction and hollowed-out relations of political representation, it reveals the proliferation of what abolitionist geographer Ruth Wilson Gilmore describes as 'organised abandonment'. A depressing mixture of 'structural adjustment, environmental degradation, privatisation, genetic modification, land expropriation, forced sterilisation, human organ theft, neocolonialism, involuntary and superexploited labor', these punishing regimes of population management would not have been possible were it not for the fundamental transformation in how capitalism itself is organised.[1]

Britain's rustbelt regions – places where heavy industry has departed and gentrification has yet to take root – have faced a kind of *disorganised* abandonment. In the wake of the 2007–8 global financial crash, Tony Blair's New Labour was succeeded by David Cameron's Conservative-led coalition. Seeking to take control of the public purse strings loosened by Gordon Brown during his bailout of Northern Rock, the Tories and their Liberal Democrat junior partners shredded the public sector to bits, radically exacerbated conditionalities on welfare claimants and encouraged the growth of cheap, insecure 'gig economy' work. They left long hospital waiting lists, bankrupt municipalities, contracted state capacity and, crucially, a poorer, sicker, lonelier population in their wake. Chapter Two names the problem. Demonstrating the decline of Britain's representative institutions and the gap between the ruler and the ruled, it asks how the neoliberal transformation of the country and its political parties was made possible by the process of class decomposition that produced both Brexit and Corbynism. It asks: how do populations respond politically to how they are managed, exploited and ruled when the system itself is undergoing a prolonged period of mounting crises?

In the absence of social-democratic state planning and with the breakdown of the neoliberal social contract, the dominance of global financial and rentier capital over the operations of British capitalism has debilitated the nation state's capacity to reproduce the conditions needed for accumulation, leaving vast swathes of the urban and bodily space of the contemporary proletariat to rot. This is seen in the conclusion of Chapter Two: the sense, predominant in the narrative of the 2024 general election, that the buses do not come frequently enough, that you cannot get a doctor's appointment or that the brickwork in your child's school is crumbling. Disorganised abandonment speaks to the fundamental contemporary 'structure of feeling' – it expresses how the citizens of this nation feel about the areas they live in.

Coined by the late cultural theorist Raymond Williams, the phrase 'structure of feeling' captures 'the felt sense of the quality of life at a particular place and time: a sense of the ways in which the particular activities combined into a way of thinking and living'.[2] Our modes of interpreting the world – before that even, of feeling it – are conditioned by the reality that neoliberal capitalism has made us lonelier than ever before and sicker than we have been for a while. The privatisation of space, the cost of life, and the physical and psychological pains of work have affected capitalism's ability to produce healthy workers. That is, workers are sick because capitalism itself feels sick. And the political right knows this better than anyone. The objects of the elites' anxiety over our demographics – our age, our ethnic background, our dwindling ability to make family units and our disdain for wage slavery – speak to the way that capitalism's contemporary problems can be boiled down to a simple, reactionary language. At this moment, the long preponderance of decline and *declinism*, as ways that political agents grasp the times, permeates the population-at-large. But, this is a long story. As early as the 1970s, Labour intellectuals and politicians such as Francis Cripps and Tony Benn laid the blame for Britain's demise as a world power at the feet of greedy financiers holding back manufacturing. Today, following in the finest traditions of Enoch Powell and British Toryism, Nigel Farage targets migrants and refugees as responsible for Britain's fall from grace, the source of a 'population explosion' which has consistently 'devalued' the lives of the seemingly indigenous citizenry. For the Faragists, inwards migration is a regrettable fact that needs to be countered with tough borders, and a domestic population working harder and making more babies. The return of the problem of population, the result of these regimes of disorganised abandonment, exemplifies how the elites' incapacity to produce the subjects they so desire has created a widespread crisis in subject formation and a subsequent set of struggles over the technologies of power used to organise and produce populations.

Long before today's crisis in population management, the rise of twentieth-century social democracy, as a civilising nationalist response to the revolutionary working-class and anticolonial movements of the interwar years, gave birth to a set of social subjects and rearticulated the lives of others. Four archetypes in particular developed a frighteningly radical potential to change the country after the Second World War. The white male Fordist car worker gradually became one of the most rebellious forces of the postwar settlement and challenged wage suppression, speed-ups and employer autocracy. The South Yorkshire miner revived traditions of industrial militancy and fought against the repeated and growing effort to crush proletarian lifeworlds constructed around the mines. The part-time female clothesmaker challenged her subordination as the domestic servant in the male-breadwinner family model and increasingly turned to uprooting forms of industrialised housework on the factory floor. The black foundry worker struggled against racist employers and exclusionary trade union bureaucracies, while questioning conditions of segregation, wage inequality and growing obsolescence. Together, these distinct subjects constituted a powerful potential coalition against an increasingly disordered postwar settlement.

The rise of Margaret Thatcher and the British New Right, the subject of the third chapter, put an end to these efforts, exploiting the crisis of postwar social democracy and disassembling the subjects which had challenged it. These radicalised Tories would mobilise a disintegrating collectivist culture, the tools of financialised management and the power of the state to crush these proletarians, absorbing some into chains of privatised social reproduction, while others would have their everyday worlds transformed beyond recognition, undeniably for the worse. For Thatcher and the New Right, some parts of the population were simply surplus to requirement.

Emerging out of the ashes of this particularly virulent brand of British conservatism, Tony Blair's New Labour sought to consolidate the Iron Lady's class war into a form of managed neoliberalism. The subject of the book's fourth chapter, New Labour cultivated a reactionary culture which demonised working-class populations, not only enforcing the low-wage, insecure forms of labour exploitation spread by Thatcher, but criminalising those who could not thrive in such a rigged economy. They demolished old working-class communities, restricted the movement of proletarians from abroad and spread the financialised networks of social reproduction to the living room through debt and mortgages, ensuring that large percentages of the population would increasingly rely on borrowing to support their family units.

In the ashes of these two regimes of late British capitalism, declinist modes of thinking have proliferated; in contrast, this book reasserts the centrality of power and capital as explanations for the population's miseries. Our pain is the product of past defeats and new dominations, and many have rationalised it by resorting to racism, gendering and mutual recrimination. Those who govern us – politicians, elites and companies – have reorganised the ways we live and breathe in order to maximise their influence and wealth, ruining the social world around us in the process. The final chapter asks the question: to what extent is Marx's claim that the working class constitutes capitalism's gravediggers still a relevant heuristic? How have successive modes of capitalism transformed the working class into a beast that is quite distinct from the social force which Marx embraced in the eighteenth century? And if substantive changes have been made, what scope today is there for a radical working-class subjectivity that can free itself from toil and oppression?

This is a tale of how we are managed precisely to make us pliant, suspicious and incapable of turning ourselves into collective subjects of radical transformation. It is an arc which traverses the contemporary breakdown of that regime in Britain. This book yearns for us to escape our collective condition together, once and for all. To begin this story, our first chapter takes us to a place I have come to call home: Stoke-on-Trent. This wonderful city, as much as any other part of this country, has experienced the sharp end of global capitalism's transformations, and offers us an insight into our past, our present and, if we fail to change things for the better, our future.

1
Marx in the Potteries

If a dog bites a man in Bond Street it is news; if a man bites a dog in Chorlton-cum-Hardy or Stoke-on-Trent it is only to be expected.

Old Fleet Street dictum

I never thought I'd end up in Stoke-on-Trent. I'm from London and, for most of my life, I hadn't even heard of the place. But, then again, maybe something in my family history prepared me for the uprooting. My granddad, Patrick, is in his seventies now, and he resides in social housing in the North West London area of Cricklewood. Patrick didn't always live in England, though. He was born in Limerick, Ireland, in the late 1940s. He belonged to a family of turf farmers, who worked mostly unprofitable farms in conditions of severe colonial de-development. Born of British imperial diktats, these conditions led to a terrible quality of life: of his ten siblings, several did not survive childhood.

When Patrick arrived in England, he moved around a lot, between Leeds, Birmingham – where he was among the team of labourers who built the original Birmingham New Street station – and eventually London, where he settled. He spent his early life as part of what used to be called 'the lump': casualised workers, disproportionately racialised minorities, earning cash in hand, living in conditions of generalised insecurity. The popular story of postwar British social-democratic glory, conveyed in Ken Loach's moving film *The Spirit of '45*, doesn't speak to the experience of folks like my granddad. That story of Keynesian demand management, improved living standards and mass council housebuilding programmes was experienced unevenly by working-class people depending on where they were from, their gender and where they lived.

After the early passing of his wife in the 1980s – and with five children to support – Patrick worked even harder, as was required of the 'lump'. And he did so precisely at the moment when workplace conditions for building workers were being eviscerated following the industrial militancy of the 1970s. He also began reproducing the bitterness which politics often trades in. Despite being subject to a culture of anti-Irish racism that saw him and his children denigrated as the undesirable social residuum and the enemy within, he bought into a story which secured him a part in the national fabric by placing his interests against black workers and those on the dole.

Michelle, Patrick's oldest daughter, experienced a radical acceleration of time: leaving school early, she took on the socially reproductive labour her mum was no longer around to do. She and her siblings spent the years when they should have been enjoying their youth trying to work through the struggles of working-class life and the trauma of losing a mother so young, in a time defined by Thatcher's war on postwar emancipatory subjects, rising unemployment and anti-Irish sentiment. These personal and political experiences were undergirded by the slow but real decline of North West London's Irish community in the 1970s and '80s: as young people uncompelled by the Catholicism of their father's homeland and surrounded by the evisceration of an immigrant moral economy built around industry, they experienced the rise of political secularism as a double-edged sword.

Of the family's five children, three would spend large parts of their life on and off the dole, on sickness benefits or in service work: products of a labour market that didn't work for them, they bore the psychological scars of neoliberalism's emergence, manifested in decades of drug abuse. The second-oldest son, followed in his father's footsteps, eking out an existence working on small, domestic construction sites. Michelle, the oldest daughter, was a single mum on benefits before she was vilified along with millions of other single mothers by John Major and then Tony Blair. She worked in chip shops, in bingo halls and – after becoming the first in the family to complete college – tirelessly as a legal secretary.

Michelle's son, I grew up in a London that was undergoing a profound set of transformations. For a time, I went to primary school on the Stonebridge estate when you could enter the concrete blocks at one end of a seventy-acre stretch and exit at the other, barely going outside but for the bridge and the precinct. Those blocks no longer exist, and many of the people who grew up on the estate live elsewhere now. I came of age in a housing association flat in Arnos Grove, before Friern Hospital – one of the country's most oppressive asylums – became Princes Park Manor, the home of Cheryl Tweedy and Ashley Cole. I lived on the Whitton Walk in Bow when residents down the road were still fighting to keep Robin Hood Gardens alive, sandwiched as they were between the oppressive shine of Canary Wharf and the rocket-propelled bluster of the Olympic Games.

Shaped by industrial contraction and de-population in the 1970s and '80s, London was, by the 1990s, undergoing a profound process of finance-led real estate regeneration. Old estates were being demolished and lifeworlds torn apart in ways evocative of the devastation of communities in Britain's rustbelt regions. London steered its way into the twenty-first century as a city reconstructed for the rich; its middling professionals and the underpaid, overworked majority of its citizens were forced to serve the wealthy while subsisting on wages which barely allowed them to cover the rent, let alone get on the property ladder.

I loved London, despite never being able to afford it, often being denied its artistic fruits and feeling depressed about being caught between the pace of city life and the complete unattainability of financial security. London gave me everyday multiculturalism, music, cheap public transport, wonderful parks, limitless crevices of surprise, the endless movement of the city and friends in abundance. But the London that made me who I am was disappearing. The intrusion of real estate and private capital into so many facets of living in London cheapened the value of life, while inflating the price of everything needed to get by.

Generally, we call this process 'gentrification'. It's a hotly contested term among geographers, campaigners and communities. The raising of housing costs; the creation of Business Improvement Districts, determined to transform city centres into playgrounds for large corporate retail chains; the substitution of local artist cultures with sterile product placement; the eradication of small, often family-owned businesses; the commodification of public spaces; and the increasing securitisation of the city against the homeless and the poor – all these combine to enact one simple goal of city elites: *Change the people*.

When I left London, initially following my wife Ingrid to her new job in Leeds, it wasn't just that I felt materially obliged to escape the city, unable to afford it unless I lived with my parents in their housing association flat into my early thirties. It was also that gentrification had turned the city I loved against me, making it impossible for me to realise a good life by transforming the metropolis I felt was my home into a complex of alienation and unaffordability. Gentrification confirms everything capitalism tells you about how inadequate you are: it confirms your inability to thrive, making it clear that there are better people than you ready to take over your city, your estate, your park and, eventually, your gaff.

I say all this to demonstrate a simple point: my exit from the city I called home was a generational process. It may even have been overdetermined. But it wasn't inevitable, and despite falling head over heels for the city of Stoke and the people who live in it, it is neither nice nor desirable to be gradually squeezed out of the place you call home. It is simply one way in which real estate magnates and city elites mould and repel historical communities in the interest of profit realisation. It is one crucial way in which working-class subjectivities, crafted over decades, are broken. The colonial disruption of lives sixty years ago – people propelled from Irish turf farms to industrial London – is intimately connected to the spatial rupture of working-class existence in the present – priced out of gentrifying London and landing in neglected Stoke-on-Trent. Making a life for myself here also meant learning that London is not the only place that offers a glimpse into our collective future.

In the late 1960s, as the optimism of postwar social democracy reached its crescendo and began to tail off, Richard Crossman toured Britain's towns and cities. Pondering the restricted possibilities which confronted urban modernism in the face of burgeoning deindustrialisation and brewing global economic challenges, the Labour housing minister was notably pessimistic. Driving through Stoke-on-Trent, dismayed at its 'ghastly collection of slag heaps, pools of water, old potteries, [and] deserted coal mines', the government official remarked that he felt 'even more strongly that it was impossible to revive Britain without letting such places as Stoke-on-Trent decline'.[1] Written an entire decade prior to Margaret Thatcher's devastating assault on working-class lifeworlds, Crossman's caustic meditations on the deteriorating state of postimperial Britain represented a crossroads moment for the type of Keynesian demand management which had endured for over twenty years.

Convinced that there was 'nothing in Stoke except the worst of the industrial revolution, and the nicest of people', Crossman and figures like him were unable and unwilling to reckon with the endemic crises confronting British society.[2] His embrace of social-democratic decline, in the face of the turmoil of global markets, led him and his successors down a path which would make the 'nicest of people' across the country – from Stoke-on-Trent's Portland Street to Tottenham's Broadwater Farm – subject to a war from above.

So what *is* Stoke-on-Trent? Located somewhat ambiguously between the West Midlands and the North of England, it is a polycentric city – the accumulation of six towns, Hanley, Stoke, Burslem, Longton, Fenton and Tunstall, alongside some smaller conurbations such as Shelton and Hartshill – with the ideology of industrialism baked into its identity. Josiah Wedgwood – grandfather to Charles Darwin and distant relative of Labour left firebrand Tony Benn – is ideologised as the effective founder of the city by way of the industry that lends Stoke its colloquial name: 'the Potteries'. The ceramics industry arose in Stoke because of the co-existence of abundant reservoirs of clay and coal throughout the North Staffordshire region, but Wedgwood restructured pottery production to capture global markets and imaginations with his Etruscan-style ceramics. Along with structural engineer James Brindley, Wedgwood presided over the opening-up of the Trent and Mersey canal, with the industrialist overseeing the construction of the historical Etruria factory village at the heart of the canal's central networks. In short, Wedgwood kickstarted the city's development as an industrial hub by auguring in a logistics revolution that opened Stoke to the world market and created an incredibly profitable ceramics industry. Today, the city's prominent heritage industry monumentalises Wedgwood, exhibiting how central the notion of capitalist benevolence is to the city's conception of itself. But real history proves far darker than the rose-tinted picture painted by the heritage industry. The ceramics capitalist's desire to develop transport routes which didn't damage his profitable earthenware plates was only made possible by canal workers – including children and migrant workers drawn from Ireland, Wales and Europe – working arduous twenty-two-hour days. In doing so, they faced abuse from local workers laid idle and forced to live on the breadline. In pottery production, workers – young, old, male and even female labourers, who were cheaper – were subjected to intensified assembly-line labour, working inhumane hours.

In his depiction of the hellscape of British industrialisation, *Capital*, Karl Marx took great interest in the potters of Staffordshire. Detailing three parliamentary inquiries into the health and conditions of child workers, Marx assembled a story of children as young as seven working fifteen-hour shifts with barely any sleep, for as little as three shillings and sixpence. The health commissioners who observed and reported on these disastrous working conditions framed the problem as one of the '"dégénérescence" of the population'; nevertheless, Marx details that lifespans drastically reduced by industrial illnesses such as potters' asthma, dyspepsia, liver and kidney disorders, and rheumatism were a product of a system of production which extracted vitality from the workers of North Staffordshire and handed money and power to the Wedgwoods of the region.[3] In fact, when Marx notoriously employs the Latin phrase 'Mutato nomine de te fabula narratur' (with the name changed, the story is about you) to compare the benevolent pieties of abolitionist British industrialists with slave drivers around the world, he is specifically paralleling the lives of potters with those of the kidnapped African slaves of Virginia and Kentucky, and the indentured servants of Ireland. It can only be deduced that Josiah Wedgwood was the Staffordshire slaver.[4]

Outside of the potbanks, Stoke's industrial history is defined by the pits. The North Staffordshire coalfields encompassed over twenty collieries: from Silverdale, Wolstanton and Chatterley Whitfield, to Sneyd Green, Hanley Deep Pit and Foxfield. In 1918, 155 coal miners died in the Minnie Pit disaster, the worst mining disaster in North Staffordshire. Women workers employed in the co-op laundry during the interwar years worked from 6am to 5pm for seven shillings a week. Industrial ailments such as lung disease and tuberculosis predominated in the city's proletarian quarters, where families with seven or eight children often lived all in one room, lacking basic amenities. The North Staffordshire Infirmary, built in 1869 and later known as the Royal Stoke Hospital, was a mainstay for a local population frequently disabled by the perils of wage slavery. Granted city status in 1925, Stoke became the first local authority to submit a five-year council housing plan under the 1930 Housing Act, expanding its supply of Victorian terraced houses under the Labour-majority city council. For those of its citizens whose industrial labour could afford such niceties, Blackpool and Southport were the region's holiday destinations of choice during the interwar years.

A holiday, for J. B. Priestley in his *English Journeys*, was the least the people of the Potteries deserved. Scornful of the region's parochialism and diminutive character, the sheer brutality of the city's factory life and the smoke 'so thick that you searched for the outbreak of fire', the novelist and playwright was 'at once repelled and fascinated by its odd appearance'.[5] Torn between his admiration for the pride that potters took in their semi-artisanal piecework, his feeling that all signs of nature's 'handiwork' had been obliterated from pottery production and his sense – as early as the 1930s – that idleness under the pressure of competition from elsewhere was repelling ceramics workers from the labour market, Priestley, like the health commissioners before him and Crossman after, struck a deeply patronising chord. His contention that 'civilised man, except in his capacity as a working potter, has not arrived here yet, just as the real city of Stoke-on-Trent, which will no doubt be a monument of civic dignity, has not yet arrived', ignored the ways in which Stokies spent the duration of their subjection to industrial capitalism fighting for a better way of life, dignity and sovereignty across the region.[6]

In the throes of the radical labour uprising known as Chartism, the Potteries area was swept up in revolt. The growth of largely illegal mining unions in the early 1830s would have a significant impact on mid-nineteenth-century Stoke. During the 1842 General Strike, the people of Burslem rose up and were fired on; nineteen-year-old shoemaker Josiah Heapey was murdered, countless others were injured, 146 demonstrators were sent to jail and 54 were deported to Australia. The event is still memorialised today by the annual Chartist festival. In 1912, a coal strike enraptured the city as part of the Great Unrest, a syndicalist rebellion of industrial workers in the lead-up to the First World War. Fourteen years later, during the 1926 General Strike, the Six Towns' proletarians shut the city down, bringing the circulation of capital to a standstill. Communist councillor Fanny Deakin fought for the people of nearby Newcastle-under-Lyme throughout the early twentieth century, campaigning for maternity care, welfare rights, miners' rights, and free milk for pregnant women and children under five. She also brought a delegation of antifascists to London to fight against Oswald Mosley's British Union of Fascists. The area's connection to radical currents stretched further afield when the film *The Proud Village*, starring world-famous communist singer and actor Paul Robeson, was filmed partly in the historical mining community of Silverdale and took on locals as extras in its production.

After the Second World War, the space and industry of the city underwent physical modernisation. The Bentilee housing estate, consisting of over 4,000 homes housing miners and steelworkers, was at one point the largest council housing estate in Europe. The Shelton Bar steelworks, formed in the nineteenth century, was nationalised in 1952. The Wolstanton 'super pit', drawing together reserves from Hanley, Sneyd Green and Chatterley Whitfield, underwent a process of modernisation, becoming the deepest pit in Western Europe. Not all modernisation bore such progressive promise, though: the Potteries Loop Line rail network – initially built in the second half of the nineteenth century, but key to creating the interconnected urban life of a new twentieth-century city – went into premature managed decline after the Second World War. The year 1963 stands out as a signal date in the long decline of the promise of urban modernism in the Potteries: the year which saw the publication of the notorious Beeching Report, which cut the Loop Line, also saw works begin on the A500 (or D Road). The dual carriageway, which rips through the middle of Stoke, connects the city to the wider region via motorway. A product of postwar motor-optimism, the construction of this road, not completely finished until 2006, was a case in point of the way that social democracy's modernisation project undermined an older, more communal industrial world. Postwar social democracy also brought with it an effort to alleviate the nation's uneven regional development. The city centre was slowly renovated during the postwar period, giving birth to modernist buildings like the Potteries Museum, the City Central Library and the brutalist BT Tower. A hotspot for culture too, Stoke-on-Trent had cinemas and theatres such as the Majestic; and until the early twenty-first century its pubs and clubs were a hub for working-class conviviality. From Northern Soul nights at The Golden Torch, and the rave scene of the early 1990s, to its vibrant indie music scene at the turn of the twenty-first century, the Potteries has until recently seen droves of people travel from far and wide to enjoy the clubs which characterised the city's rich cultural tapestry.

But this lifeworld, built around industry, evoked in the city's forever-busy workingmen's clubs, was eventually turned upside down. As the buoyant optimism of the 1960s gave way to global economic upheaval, and the workers' militancy of the early 1970s confronted industrial contraction, increasingly vulnerable industrial workers in the mines, steelworks and diminishing potbanks were put into positions where they were fighting not just for wage increases, renewed power and shopfloor autonomy, but for the continued existence of their very livelihoods and social worlds. Nowhere was this clearer than at Shelton Bar. Ted Smith, a shop steward helping to lead the struggle to save jobs in the early 1970s, later a council leader and the inspiration for the famous *Steelman* sculpture, would not have any of the same success in saving the steelworks from closure later in the decade, despite the workforce partnering with management to seek an alternative plan for the firm.

Manufacturing output as a share of British gross domestic product (GDP) shrank between 1979 and 2025 by 23 per cent, while national manufacturing employment collapsed by roughly 60 per cent. A product of global competition, and later Thatcher's war on industrial workers, this assault from above had a profound impact on the fabric of society across the Potteries. Rose Hunter, prominent member of the North Staffs Miner's Wives Action Group (NSMWAG), conveys this story in intimate detail. The child of a Pakistani miner who migrated from Scotland to Stoke-on-Trent when she was young, Rose grew up in a trade union family. Her mother was a union representative at Polarcold in Congleton; as a young woman, Rose married a miner and settled on a miners' estate where she still lives today, having bought the house directly from the National Coal Board. A trade unionist in her own right, Rose organised at work as a nurse and as a garment worker, and raised a family before getting involved in the 1984–5 miners' strike. Appalled by the scenes of violent police abuse against miners at the

Battle of Orgreave, and after giving birth to her second son, Rose recounts the chaos of turning up to her first NSMWAG meeting. Going along to a workshop on the strip searches of Irish Republican women, meeting campaign founder Brenda Proctor for the first time, feeling completely sucked in by the energy of these militant women, miners' wives and feminists, Rose remembers that she 'just wanted more of it'.

Notably, Rose refuses to see the strike as a defeat because it involved a whole community who 'fought everything that was thrown against us'. Nevertheless, she is honest that it 'wasn't easy for a lot of people … it was a bit scary as well, as in fuck's sake, you know, how's this gonna all end up?' Despite the enormity of the resistance throughout the country, across pit villages and in solidarity movements further afield, the strike ended up with the miners going back to work. By the turn of the century, Stoke-on-Trent – once one of Britain's industrial centres, employing tens of thousands of miners after the Second World War and 50,000 potters in the 1970s – employed fewer than 5,000 ceramics workers and no miners. Although, as Rose makes clear, 'everyone was devastated' after the miners' strike, she remembers the agency that the men exercised in organising to defend their communities from obliteration as being a beginning, not an end: speaking of the miners' wives, she recalls, 'this was a start for us'. As well as co-organising the Trentham Colliery Pit occupation in 1993, Rose would go on to support struggles against South African Apartheid, the deportation of migrants, strikes by other workers and much else. The miners' struggle against Thatcherism fuelled Rose's fire, and the strikers' loss did not dampen it.

But the bleeding of Stoke's industrial base also correlated with efforts to transform the city's infrastructure into saleable assets in the absence of a sound financial footing for municipal development. Privatisation had to face down local attempts to cling to the older associational life that this civic infrastructure had underpinned. A long protest by residents in the 1980s to preserve Longton Town Hall was a rare success, but the direction of travel was indicated when the North Staffordshire railway was closed and built over in the latter half of the century, just like the Potteries Loop Line before it. As deindustrialisation took hold, the wasteland which encircled Etruria – Wedgwood's factory town – was transformed under Thatcher into the site of one of her Garden Festivals. These festivals were a pillar of Thatcher's effort to lure private investment back into postindustrial spaces in need of urban regeneration and to transform the spaces of Britain's rustbelt regions. In Stoke's case, this was the city's third attempt at obtaining national economic support after being rejected in its applications for designation as an enterprise zone and as an assisted area. And the outcome of this vaunted process of postindustrial renewal? By the mid-1990s, the birthplace of Stoke's industrial history had become Festival Park: a retail park offering cheap services for its customers and low pay for its staff, sucking consumption out of the city's high streets and town centres.

The process of unmaking an associational life – at once spatial, social and economic – constitutes what Dominic Davies has described in *The Broken Promise of Infrastructure* as an 'infrastructure of feeling'.[7] Stoke's physical space, devastated by deindustrialisation, Thatcherism's efforts to transform postindustrial spaces into renewed sites for extraction and exploitation through new industries such as logistics, and then the austerian years of David Cameron and George Osborne's Conservative-led coalition, all embodied the 'spatial imprisonment' of the city's people. Former postal worker and trade unionist Joe McCluskey captures the twinned sense of repetition and crisis contained in the loss of the city's associational life. Recalling the nostalgic stories his older colleagues on the post told him when he was 19 years old about how Hanley was when they were his age, when 'you used to have to wear a shirt and tie in a pub ... and you could go on a night out around Longton', Joe remarked to me that he now finds himself recounting similar stories to his niece on an even grimmer scale. 'It's not that bad that you can't buy the clothes and the shoes and the bags or you know the material items that you want,' Joe argues, 'but in terms of like the social side ... fucking dead ... I don't know if I'd use the term managed decline either. I think it's just been forgotten.' Collapsing transport, segregated and abandoned local economies, and a shrinking safety net have all contributed not just towards a sense of decline, but towards a reality of *disorganised* abandonment, in which the coping strategies of disempowered municipalities have left vast swathes of the city's physical life to rot.

The constant clamour for regeneration from the city's elites is a contributing factor to the profound pessimism people feel about the present and future of Stoke. People hear state bureaucrats, Treasury officials and politicians speak of municipal improvements, but they see £1 million in cuts to children's centres of the kind made by the Labour-run council in 2017, resulting in closures and staffing losses. They see the 2016 city council investment of £3.4 million into the Etruria Valley link, or 'Silicon Stoke', with little to no benefit for their communities, but breaks on business rates for capitalist firms. They observe the city council give money and subordinate itself to the whims of private sector job creation in the form of services and warehouses, with no resulting benefits for the people these corporations employ, most notably in the form of wages. And most recently they see, with great frustration, the site of the stalled Etruscan Square development in Hanley, now projected to be luxury flats, while the half-empty Home Office and DWP buildings that surround it remind the city's residents of the misplaced priorities of our rulers. As Joe argues, 'That's the thing about the 2008 recession, where people go on about, you know, have we recovered yet?

Has the country recovered yet? I don't think we recovered from whatever the recession was before then. You know what I mean? We used to have like six town centres. Then we had one. Now we've got barely one.'

Perhaps what feels like old hat in towns like Stoke is the future elsewhere. Sacha Hilhorst's contention, in 'A Tale of Two Towns', that postindustrial towns and cities such as Mansfield and Corby have become sites of innovative labour regimes, foreshadowing new locuses of spatial exploitation and transformation, suggests as much. As Hilhorst astutely documents, the Treasury under both Tony Blair and the Cameron-era Tories played a numbers game across the nation's rustbelt regions, facilitating the creation of insecure, intensified forms of labour exploitation in exchange for money to be invested privately, in the coffers of private retail, care and logistics firms, alongside real estate.[8] But it does beg the question: who is included and excluded from these new, localised regimes of power and exploitation, and how do they reinforce the deep-seated sense people in Stoke have that they have been abandoned?

We exited Stoke station with a feeling of nervous excitement. Ingrid walked us to the taxi she'd booked and nattered with the driver as we drove to our new home. We were relocating to Stoke-on-Trent and I could hear her accent turn up a notch in conversation with this local Burslemite. We talked about Port Vale FC's incipient rise to the top of League Two. He told us how tetchy local derbies used to be when the Vale and Stoke City would meet, a rare phenomenon now they play in different divisions. For most of our drive, he was a calming presence in this journey out of my comfort zone. After a few minutes of talking to him, I was warming to the place and the people. 'We've had hard times,' he said, 'but we have a knack for pulling through.'

But when we told him where we were moving to, that all changed. A cautionary tone took hold of his voice. Since he was dropping us off in Hanley town centre, the informal heart of Stoke's Six Towns, he hadn't realised the estate we were moving into. He warned us of how far downhill it had gone, how rough it was and the kind of characters which haunted it. The happy expression melted from his face, replaced by something more sombre. As he pulled up outside the Potteries Museum, after apprising us of the dodgy individuals who inhabited our new area, he sent us off on our way with a forlorn 'Good luck!'

Walk onto the estate I now call home and you'll see an abandoned wasteland at the bottom of Century Street, shrouded in overgrown weeds over twice the height of a tall human being. If you look closely enough on a bright day, you can spot the skeletons of the old pottery infrastructure this new wildlife has claimed as its own. Once the site of a succession of potbanks and then the chemical company Century Oils, this abandoned wasteland sits across from the remaining oil refinery site, owned for several decades by Fuchs Lubritech. The walk I do almost every other day – sandwiched between this oil refinery and an abandoned, potentially oil-contaminated wasteland – is a searing reminder of what has become of contemporary Britain. The Fuchs site caters to a smaller workforce, almost exclusively from outside the area, and provides the local residents with the added benefit of living in a very loud blast zone.

This is an area that has undergone wave after wave of deindustrialisation. The closure of the potbanks – like the transformation of Shelton Bar into one of Margaret Thatcher's Garden Festivals and then into a retail park – speaks to the layering of different moments of worker obsolescence manifest in the space of the city. The global wave of manufacturing overcapacity which successively undermined the British industrial economy – decreasing the share of workers employed in steel, mining and mills – can still be felt today in Stoke-on-Trent. Devastatingly so on my estate. In the decades since this wasteland was created, there has been plenty of time for literally *anything* to occur on this land. Instead, this possibly oil-contaminated space has become part junkyard, part encampment for the area's vulnerable drug users and homeless people. The potential purchase of the land for housing, secured some five years ago by renewables investment firm Bluefield Sandbach, was thrown up in the air in 2024 when the Forestry Commission demanded the developers plant 410 trees on the site. Bluefield Sandbach, which initially offered up a measly 25 per cent of the proposed units for 'affordable housing' with absolutely no guarantee of social rents, has been locked in a protracted legal stalemate.

Rebecca Davies, local visual artist, co-directs the Portland Inn Project, a creative arts community project based on the estate. A Londoner who 'had a lot of beef about regeneration and gentrification' in her native Elephant and Castle, Rebecca left the capital after 'really struggling to afford to live' there, and moved to Stoke-on-Trent. Rebecca connected with Stoke, her mother's hometown, through the Oasis Social Club, part entertainment venue, part discussion space, incorporating the long British tradition of working men's clubs. Inspired by the kinds of working-class socialities found in spaces like her granddad's workingmen's club in Coventry, and worried about their slow erosion, she toured places like Stoke, East London, Hull and Preston, using her artistic practice to recreate characters like the pub landlady and tapping into the breadth and depth of working-class creativity and conviviality.

When she came across the Portland Street estate, she recognised a community, like her own in Elephant and Castle, that had been shut out of decision-making and which had resisted efforts at social cleansing. In the case of the Portland estate, it had been the Pathfinder scheme. Labour grandee John Prescott had offered the estate up as a site for the scheme, as part of an effort to clear the nation's postindustrial 'sink estates' of their undeserving poor. Resistance by locals, able to lean on the area's heritage status, ultimately prevented this sordid outcome. Instead, Stoke-on-Trent City Council sought to engineer the area's population by other means. Through its £1 house scheme, the council sought to convince young, professional Stokies who had left the city to come back, in the hope that they would bring their skills (and hopefully their spending power) to regenerate and gentrify the area. Although a handful of people took this scheme up, embraced the estate and made it their own, others left and the scheme ultimately failed. According to Rebecca, 'It was quite palpable just how exhausted people were in this neighbourhood of like consultation and like we called it sort of consultation fatigue that it's just like constant questions, but actually not really, nothing really happening from it.' After repeatedly neglecting and putting down the estate, the council eventually claimed that the £1 housing scheme was creating community tensions between new residents and the longstanding residents of the estate. In response, Rebecca, her fellow co-director Anna Francis and a board of local representatives sought to combat this tension by developing a community manifesto which demanded a space for the community to share. Eventually, the council responded and handed over the keys to the Portland Inn building, laying the groundwork for the project itself. Today, the pub is on the cusp of reopening as a renovated community centre for the estate's residents.

Named a 'Grot Spot' by local newspaper the *Sentinel*, the two-up, two-down estate which surrounds Portland Street is subjected to a level of classed and racialised vilification which mirrors the treatment of the ghettos of the United States and the banlieues of suburban Paris. A poster pinned on the wall outside the dilapidated Caterchoice warehouse, made by a young resident whose house backs onto steel plate firm Brown McFarlane, declares, 'We want oxygen!' Evoking the Black Lives Matter slogan, 'We can't breathe', which came to prominence just two years earlier, the poster speaks to the ways in which this multiracial working-class community has been abandoned, declared undeserving of clean air and – as Rebecca makes clear – subject to 'industrial gaslighting' by the Fuchs Lubritech company, which tells defiant residents their concerns about air quality are 'in your mind, you know this, there's no smell here'. The estate is one of the most multicultural areas in the city, and so it is no surprise to Rebecca that 'so much of that decision-making and that sort of marginalising of people's lives is so rooted in kind of prejudice of working-class people or immigrant families, refugee families, people of colour'.

The Portland Inn Project's efforts at developing a different vision of art-centred community empowerment has combined with locals that have learned the hard way that they must fight for themselves in the face of abandonment. Well under half of the estate's residents are owner-occupiers and mortgage holders – most rent privately or through social housing. Purposefully shut off from the centre of Hanley on whose edges it sits, the estate is rife with homelessness and drug abuse, much of which the police and Business Improvement District have directed away from the city centre. As Isaac Rose has succinctly documented in the Mancunian case, this process emulates US urban regeneration strategies that aim to attract high earners while cleansing public space of the undeserving. Absentee landlords, landlords exploiting their tenants and forcing them into mouldy houses in multiple occupation (HMOs), high rates of unemployment and widespread gig economy work all proliferate.

The bad rap this nice taxi driver gave the place we were about to embrace as our home reflects the stories told of the city by the press, politicians and even many of its own citizens. The iLiveHere poll of over 100,000 people across the country has had Stoke on the list of top ten 'worst places to live in UK' several times, and popular vlogger Billy Moore regularly travels to different parts of Stoke, which he labels 'monkey dust city', speaking mostly to drug users about the city's problems.[9] Jane Ashworth, current leader of the Labour-run city council, told the *Financial Times* on entering office, 'We knew it was bad. But we had no idea it was this bad.' Referring to the fiscal constraints imposed on the council as a result of government funding cuts amounting to 26.9 per cent in real-terms spending, Ashworth remarked, 'There is just less that you can cut … It can't be good for people's self-worth if the back streets are filthy and the heritage buildings are falling apart.'[10]

According to the Care Quality Commission, Stoke is the thirteenth most deprived place in England and the Special Interest Group of Municipal Authorities reports that it is in the top 10 per cent of deprived local authorities. Municipalities such as Stoke-on-Trent City Council, hemmed in by Thatcherism's disempowerment of local government, teeter on the brink of bankruptcy, spending vast sums on care, schools and social services. The concomitant processes of deindustrialisation and austerity mean that local government is more often than not an institution for presiding over decline.

According to Sacha Hilhorst, to depict places like Stoke-on-Trent as being 'left behind' misses the point. Since the early days of Margaret Thatcher's premiership, politicians have sought to remake Britain's postindustrial towns by utilising them as 'testing grounds for successive waves of neoliberal policymaking'.[11] Combining entrepreneurial regeneration strategies with the facilitation of low pay, insecurity and minimal workplace rights, the nation's former industrial hubs have, Hilhorst argues, become the sites of capitalist innovation. Care work, financialisation, logistics and free enterprise zones coalesce to forge the country's future rather than its past. Rather than being 'left behind', towns and cities like the Potteries have been opened up to new configurations of power and exploitation.[12]

When you come off the A50 onto the A500, traversing the much-vaunted A50/A500 'industrial corridor' that connects the East Midlands with its western counterpart, you are entering a world of manufacturing occupied by Toyota, Rolls-Royce and JCB. Employing the small units of better-paid workers that circle the Staffordshire region, these precious secure jobs are a bug of the local economy, not a feature. These workers constitute the outer rim of Hal Draper's 'concentric circles', the geographical form of exploitation and reproduction pulling the vast majority of Stoke's workers into its productive orbit.[13] With logistics and service workers at its heart, this Midlands city relies on the movement of commodities, creating a diverse, spatially conditioned and often super-exploited workforce. One of the hearts of Britain's supply chain structure, the city and its surrounding areas, with their 16,400 logistics and distribution workers, are assembled in clusters and nodes, attending to capital's needs on a grand scale and embracing 'just-in-time' lean management production methods. In this way, employers subject workers to intensified bouts of exploitation, meeting thirty-minute timeframes which 'eliminate waste' at the expense of people's time, bodies and psyches.

The existence of scaled-down industrial firms on the city's periphery does not equal success for the city's former manufacturing strongholds, though. In April 2025, after 100 years of production, pottery firm Moorcroft announced its closure, but followed this with confirmation that it would in fact be saved. Earlier that year, Royal Stafford had gone bust after 200 years. Ceramics worker Rob Morley, who has worked for eight different ceramics factories in the Staffordshire area since his teenage years, told the *Guardian*, 'They're all going, bit by bit. There's going to be none left in Stoke-on-Trent, and we're supposed to be the Potteries.'[14] In September 2025, it was declared that the famous Wedgwood factory would undergo a pause in production due to low demand. A protest organised by the workers in the GMB trade union – and supported by Labour MP Gareth Snell – insisted on government protection for the British ceramics industries, but was unable to protect local industry from the double whammy of rising energy costs and an increasingly competitive global market. The profound sense of decline which takes hold of Stoke is deeply related to the collapse of the industry its historical identity is so bound up with. Underpinning this decline is the extent to which Stoke-on-Trent typifies a transformation in the world of work, from a past of pottery production, to a present and future of health, services and logistics.

This feeling of having been 'left behind' is also informed by the physical health of the city's working-class population. On a visit to the Bentilee housing estate in a rural corner of Stoke-on-Trent, I was struck by two images. First, an unavoidable eyesore – a house adorned by a Trump 2024 flag– followed by three houses each receiving a visit from a health professional. Then, amid a sea of semi-detached 'sunhouses', the Bentilee Neighbourhood Centre: a private finance initiative health centre overflowing with people walking in and out. Bentilee is the poorest place in Stoke: workers here earn £10,000 less every year than those in Stoke's richest areas. Unlike other parts of this city, in which low wages are sustained by low house prices, Bentilee is not dominated by private homeownership. Bentilee's history and spatial makeup are unique in many respects, but in two key ways it is indicative of a developing picture throughout Britain. Most of its working residents are employed in care, health and 'elementary occupations' and they suffer a lower life expectancy and poorer health than their counterparts across the city. As Gabriel Winant has recently tracked in the US case, in former industrial areas, the work of caring for sick and broken bodies becomes more and more dominant, even though those doing the work are often the same people whose sickness and exhaustion feeds the growing industry.[15] A person's place in the nation's hierarchy of class power can be read increasingly through the lens of health outcomes, which tell a story about where you live and what job you do.

For Stoke, this is a story of a class war lost, the effect of which is reflected in the state of the population's health. Child poverty rates are as high as 33.3 per cent, and free school meals eligibility rates are higher than the national average; the Potteries is one of the worst areas in the country for loss of years to pancreatic cancer and chronic obstructive pulmonary disease, and its citizens are significantly more likely to lose a higher number of years of life to lung cancer and coronary heart disease than the national average. Altogether, it is little wonder that preventable mortality is 215 per 100,000 compared with the English average of 142 per 100,000. The NHS Stoke Clinical Commissioning Group revealed in 2022 that the life expectancy of the most deprived residents in Staffordshire is about eight years lower than that of the least deprived citizens. These trends came to a head in the COVID-19 pandemic, which saw infection rates in Stoke as high as 5,220 per 100,000 and death rates at 182 per 100,000, compared with 3,430 infections and 92 deaths per 100,000 in the South East of England.

This violent situation has wider implications for the political economy and culture of Stoke-on-Trent. The city boasts an economic inactivity rate higher than the English average (and the highest in the West Midlands), and those involved in reproductive work attend in part to the needs of their peers in a health and social care industry which has become deeply commodified since the city's modernist heyday. Of all paid workers, demand for nurses is highest (followed by heavy goods vehicle drivers), and the health and social work industry is the largest in the city, consisting of seventy-nine care homes and Royal Stoke Hospital, one of the largest hospitals in the country, which employs 11,000 workers across its two sites. The toll of working in a hospital or a care home – attending to multiple patients, lifting, cleaning and feeding them, and saving their lives, all under conditions of relatively low pay for nurses, and profoundly exploitative labour regimes for migrant care workers – creates a rampant feedback loop. It destroys the bodies of workers while increasing the burdens on a strained, under-resourced health system. This dynamic is fuelled by the reality that, like the rest of the country, Stoke has an ageing population. Healthy life expectancy for males and females is four and five years lower than the national average respectively. Moreover, Stoke is not immune from the 'brain drain' which afflicts large parts of the North, with almost half of Northerners aged between sixteen and twenty-one expecting to leave their hometowns in search of better employment prospects.

The conditions of reproducing life are incredibly constrained in Stoke-on-Trent. With some of the highest rates of low-paid, low-skilled work and poverty in the country, it may be no wonder. Some 72 of the city's 159 neighbourhoods, including my own, were among the 20 per cent most income-deprived in the country. Additionally, five out of every ten people in Stoke-on-Trent are living in the most deprived areas of the country (compared with two out of ten nationally). Yet, despite high levels of economic precarity and inactivity that suggest the fragmentation of an older working-class life, it is clear that by any metric Stoke remains a working-class city. The neighbour who struggles to leave their house because of their physical and psychological ailments; members of my community arriving home in the early hours of the morning having worked insecure, zero-hours contracts; and older women using walking sticks as they monitor the self-checkout tills in Morrisons: these are the subjects that make up the contemporary working class. And it is in no small part because of their subordination by a very modern regime of work that Stoke's people suffer such physical, psychological and social decline.

This regime is reflected in the relationship between health, work insecurity and welfare. Fourteen per cent of the working-age population in Stoke claim a disability which affects their everyday life. Already eighteenth among the top-fifty local authorities that have undergone benefit reductions as a result of welfare reforms, Stoke was branded the 'debt capital of England and Wales' in 2018 due to a high rate of individual insolvencies between 2017 and 2019. Today, even those on average full-time salaries of £30,000 a year are struggling with the rising cost of food, rent and basic goods. Between 2021 and 2022, the period of time which saw the energy price cap lifted and big supermarkets and suppliers resort to 'greedflation' in response to war and climate change-induced shocks to global supply chains, Citizens Advice Staffordshire North and Stoke-on-Trent saw a 52 per cent increase in enquiries over debt and a 191 per cent increase in enquiries around utilities and communications. If one homes in on my own ward, Hanley and Etruria, almost 26 per cent of the population is on Universal Credit, with a quarter of those people in work, and a large portion of them facing the government's increasingly punitive conditionality regime.

Despite owner-occupation being the most common form of housing tenure across classes within the city, the conditions of life for the majority are shaped by indebtedness. This is the case for private renters, social housing residents and those, like myself, paying high-interest-rate mortgages. The council housing stock of 17,500 homes is among the largest in the West Midlands, but still by no means large enough to service the impoverished citizenry of the Potteries area. Thatcher's Right to Buy may have been taken up at scale by residents in areas such as Meir and Longton, but in communities such as Hanley and Shelton, with large racialised minorities, high degrees of housing segregation and big working-class populations, the predominance of private renting in particular is far greater. While the role of older, homeowning retirees is a critical component in the wider breakdown of Labour's electoral fortunes in this city, Stoke-on-Trent is, like many of the country's large urban areas, still a place where landlords run riot over the city's propertyless proletarians. Average monthly rents across the city increased by 10.8 per cent between July 2024 and July 2025, but there has been neither a correlative uptick in the quality of housing, nor a concomitant increase in real wages. No-fault evictions across the city shot up in 2024, consuming 70 per cent of the Citizens Advice Bureau's housing support team's time, with one woman, Susan, being kicked out of the house she had lived in for thirty years simply because the landlord wanted to sell. Not content with taking their tenants to court, some landlords have locked them out and forced them to live in their cars, while others box their tenants, who are often migrant workers, into illegal and pest-infested HMOs. The growth in landlordism across the city, of inattentive and exploitative housing and building proprietors, has warped the city's physical space. Building owners sit on empty properties, often refusing works or unappealing purchase offers, and in the process they leave colossal amounts of the city's brownfield land vacant. This compounds the overriding local perception that the city has been left to rot by the rich and powerful. At its most cruel, despite so many unoccupied buildings, the Labour-run Stoke-on-Trent City Council in 2017 proffered the idea that homeless people found sleeping in tents in the city centre could be fined up to £1,000. The current council, under Ashworth's leadership, made good on that reactionary sentiment by mobilising the Staffordshire police to tear down six rough-sleeper camps in the space of two weeks.

The sense of 'left behindness' which characterises so much of contemporary political discourse resonates precisely because people in places like Stoke feel the contours of organised abandonment. On my own estate, you can see the melting pot of shit, precaritised jobs, appalling housing conditions, stark images of abandonment caught in the bonfires lit on winter nights to warm the homeless and poor, and the ghosts of neoliberalism's wars in the form of drug addiction. Sam Wetherell's insight that 'those who have been abandoned by capital, do also abandon themselves' speaks to the spread of loneliness, addiction, bad health and social atomisation prevalent across the city.[16]

Nowhere is this image more pertinent than in Stoke's ongoing drug crisis: an epidemic of 'monkey dust' use that straddles a precarious line between public health emergency and moral panic. This reality tells us much about how the dynamics of abandonment shape the real and imagined experience of class in the twenty-first century. When I walk past the seemingly vacant Caterchoice industrial warehouse unit, into the alley which links our estate to Hanley Forest Park, I am suddenly sandwiched between two sites of abandonment. In both the industrial warehouse and the vacant wasteland directly across from it, homeless drug users, often addicted to monkey dust but with a range of other dependencies too, regularly set up camp, sleep and use in these empty spaces. It isn't a rarity to see a queue of users leaking impatiently out of the back alley across from my home, awaiting their next pick up or spiralling into what looks like a hallucinatory episode.

Usually the product of cathinone-class MDPHP, monkey dust speeds up the interactions between the body and brain in a similar fashion to cocaine and MDMA, but it can be easily and cheaply purchased, making it an ideal drug trade commodity in a poor transit city such as Stoke. Of the seventy-five deaths involving a synthetic cathinone recorded in Britain between 2019 and 2023, 52 per cent happened in Staffordshire, according to a 2025 Advisory Council on the Misuse of Drugs report. Once £2-a-hit, the synthetic psychoactive substance drags users into a paranoid, hallucinatory and erratic state, intensifying the symptomatic social conditions in which it thrives. It is often said that those who abuse it can be violent, and while I do not doubt that – I take seriously the fear the children and parents in our community feel in the face of open use – there is also an incredible vulnerability to those trapped in its thrall. Former Conservative MP for Stoke-on-Trent South Jack Brereton's claim that monkey dust transformed its users into 'zombies', according to reports from his constituents, is symptomatic of a criminalisation approach towards drug abuse that is growing in popularity. But it ignores a fundamental reality underlying the drugs boom in Stoke. These people are in many ways *our* people, sometimes even the grandchildren of ex-industrial workers, ruined by the matrix of factors affecting everyone in the city. The moral panic about the 'zombie' chimes precisely because underlying it for the large majority is a sense that, were the wrong move made in *our* lives, a mistake, or a crisis unbeknown to us, many of us may not be too far from being sucked in by the range of processes which push people towards monkey dust addiction. It is a fear of what could be, as well as what is. In Stoke-on-Trent, we confront Marxist geographer Henri Lefebvre's reworking of the concept of 'arrythmia', trying to subsist in an anxious social world, out of beat, out of lockstep with each other, and continuously sickened, disabled or depressed by a social system which dominates and exploits us.

And underpinning it is a pervasive hopelessness: social harms are warehoused away in the city's ghettos, or in the network of eight prisons which surround this postindustrial city. Everybody's worth is contingent on their availability to capital, and those who have been deemed disposable – a burden to the system-at-large, or inconsistently hyper-exploitable – are drawn into the process of profit-making at a moment's notice, with little ability to determine their own lives. This city can be an incredibly tough place. Homelessness rose by 28 per cent between 2022/23 and 2023/24 and the city scores a miserable 77.9 for suicides according to the national Health Index. In 1989, coping with the strains of chronic illness, drug abuse and mass unemployment, Stoke was labelled a 'sick city'.[17] Since then, subject to new forms of domination and exploitation, and with many of its citizens made surplus to requirements, it has experienced deeper wells of abandonment, and an even deeper sense of decline. Today, Stoke-on-Trent is a city of sick proletarians.

The city currently lies at a crossroads, however. Absent the will or strategy to escape Thatcher's restrictions on the ability of councils to democratically raise revenue, one of the options that appeals to right-wing Labour council groups consists of totally accepting neoliberal constraints and courting and consolidating wealthier populations through property development and gentrification. But it is challenging to redevelop and fill in what Neil Smith describes as the 'rent gap' – the space between what landlords currently earn and what they feel they *could* earn – when your city meets none of the requirements that facilitated such processes in the country's large cities.[18]

Simply put, Stoke-on-Trent does not have the infrastructure. The scrapping of the HS2 high-speed rail line beyond Birmingham put a severe dampener on recent attempts to create a gentrified core of better-paid professionals coming and going between Birmingham, Manchester and the city. The Capital and Centric Goods Yard development behind Stoke rail station, disengaged from the broader cultural and social fabric of the city, serves this purpose somewhat. And the announcement that the same firm will be appointed to regenerate the former Spode factory just minutes away from the station epitomises the grasp for a gentrification strategy among municipal elites, potentially reproducing Capital and Centric's social cleansing of the arts community from Manchester's Crusader Mill. But when it comes to the perpetual song and dance about what the council will do with the derelict brownfield land across the city, stasis prevails, because few residents can afford to live in luxury apartments or spend shedloads of money in shopping malls.

Shifting away from the strictly cultural depiction of places like Stoke-on-Trent which predominates in mainstream narratives, we should ask ourselves a meaningful question about the city and the region's place in the geography of British capitalism. The answer to this question should not be taken for granted. The Potteries has always occupied a transitory location in the circuits connecting distinct parts of national and imperial capitalism, embodying the contradictions and tensions of the system's advanced and declining forms. Today is no different.

Stoke and the region orbiting it resemble Phil A. Neel's 'near hinterlands', with the rural space of the region and the texture of the city's postindustrial landscape being consciously recreated as clusters of value production, logistics nodes and relatively large state bureaucracies. These sit beside, are dependent on and are ultimately conducive to large, vulnerable, superfluous populations that are increasingly reliant on the local state; contemporary slum neighbourhoods; a shrinking tax base; and forms of abandonment expressed in the proliferation of drug abuse and rustbelt illegality. North Staffordshire's complex logistics networks and access to the A500 corridor, connecting Birmingham to Manchester, modifies our understanding of what constitutes the core of contemporary British capitalism. For as much as the country's large financialised, creative cities dominate our conception of what 'advanced' means today, these are, in Neel's words, only the 'tip of an economic iceberg', impossible without the broader matrix of social relations in the 'near hinterlands', the 'black depths' or the 'complex mesh of infrastructure which links them together'.[19]

In many ways, it does not make sense to label this city – which produces workers, profit, industry and capitalist power relations – as postindustrial. But then how can the image ever be escaped, when you experience the absence of the city's historic industries right across its landscape? Terry McGee's notion of 'Desakota', combining the ghosts of older forms of productivity with newer ones, speaks to the reality that Britain's postindustrial towns and cities are actually quite complex. As Christina Beatty and Steve Fothergill have remarked, rustbelt regions like the Potteries are large in number, encompass city centres, rural peripheries and often smaller former mining towns, and account for roughly 16 million people, or 23 per cent of the national population. Stoke-on-Trent asks us not only to question our conceptions of future and past, or core and periphery – it also demands that we rethink the pressures shaping contemporary capitalism.

Capitalist firms such as bet365, JCB and Vodafone take advantage of cheap labour conditions, paying a minority of their workforce relatively decent wages which would cost a fortune in larger cities because of the growing real estate bubble and the increased costs of social reproduction, particularly housing. These employers, like much of Stoke's business class, have an interest in low house and rental prices precisely because costly social reproduction creates greater friction within the workplace and jeopardises the existing labour market model. The domination of strict labour regimes, with access to agile, readily available labour supplies that are disproportionately racialised and gendered, is a staple of the city's labour market. The region's mash-up of old and new industrial forms is also evocative of Russian Marxist Leon Trotsky's notion of 'uneven and combined development', where new processes of commodification rationalise precarious and stable labour to service the city, and connect the vast hubs of capitalist circuitry. Not in a cogent, composite way which transforms Stoke into a place like Manchester or London, but rather in a way which combines 'advanced' and 'backwards' social forms, birthing new class relations and distinct social subjects.

Stoke-on-Trent City Council, however, while incentivised by the impositions of the British state to facilitate this complex set of social relations, are hit by two dawning realisations. On the one hand, it isn't a city they're governing and recreating, but a range of transitory class constellations designed to service capital and its dynamics across the West Midlands and the Trent. On the other hand, the expanding Mancunian real estate bubble, the cost of transport for workers and the growing unattainability of homeownership in the Northern Powerhouse make it increasingly difficult for workers to live there. This is inciting property developers to spread their wings to the towns and cities which span the course of the M6 – among them, Stoke-on-Trent.

While the twin process of overaccumulation and spatial fixing dramatically undermined Stoke-on-Trent's industrial base, in other parts of the country this has created the conditions for what David Harvey has called 'capital switching'. At the turn of the twenty-first century, across London, Manchester, Liverpool and other large cities, capital absorbed large surpluses by switching their investments from production-centred sites to real estate speculation. This transformed the built environment of these cities, after the industrial contraction and depopulation of the 1970s and '80s, into new sites for the coordination of real estate expansion and extraction, and the priorities of municipalities such as the Greater London Authority were modified to align with this shift. By the 2000s, growing corporate profits painted over the reality that money was being diverted from productive fixed capital investment into property, the built environment and construction. For the private sector and pension funds in particular, as geographer Brett Christophers tentatively details, direct investment both 'increased their exposure to the property investment sector' and severely reduced their exposure to forms of industrial production facing persistent crises of overaccumulation throughout the 1990s.[20] In Manchester, as Isaac Rose has convincingly demonstrated, it was the Labour council that embraced this 'entrepreneurial revolution' and opened up urban regeneration and private investment to developers such as Urban Splash, Capital & Centric and the Abu Dhabi United Group which took over Manchester City Football Club in 2008.

Today, in Stoke, we're witnessing the incipient spread of this phenomenon. The 2008 financial crash, which devastated livelihoods and was taken as the pretext for the Conservative austerity regime, deepened the loss of jobs and businesses, scarring the high streets of the Six Towns in the process. As David Harvey has written, the financial crash should also 'be understood as an urban crisis, not just a financial crisis; it is a financial crisis of urbanization'.[21] So, while capital switching was a real phenomenon in the 2000s and 2010s, what we're witnessing here is not switching between two different forms of money circulation, but instead the spread of the Manchester Model, predicated on some of the largest variations between rich and poor in the country, to Stoke-on-Trent.

The developing alliance between Capital and Centric and Stoke-on-Trent's Labour-led city council is attempting to embark on this process in my new hometown, and it concerns me deeply. While the council's 2024–8 Economic Development Strategy makes some decent noises about rejuvenating the city's public space, experimenting with community asset transfers and increasing social wealth, the overwhelming focus of city regeneration has been private-led development. If we take the Goods Yard site as an example, the renovation of the surrounding area is welcome, but the council celebrating the creation of 174 rental apartments, all more than £200 above the average rental price for single-occupancy tenures, seems to be reconstituting who the city is and is not available to. Rather than charting an independent developmental course for the city that will improve its citizens' quality of life, the city municipality is turning Stoke into a satellite town for neighbouring cities that have undergone real estate–led regeneration, with emboldened property developers now on the prowl for sites where expensive housing can be built for better-off workers employed in places like Manchester and Birmingham. Of the nearly 5,000 homes being built in plans approved by Stoke-on-Trent City Council (a negligible proportion of which are genuinely social housing), many are oriented towards the city's connections to elsewhere. The Goods Yard, the Spode site, the former Olympus Engineering site on College Road, Booth Street in Stoke town and the former Royal Stoke Hospital car park site just up the road are all examples of a city strategy geared towards making Stoke-on-Trent into a commodified tourist hub, on the one hand, and a satellite for rapidly changing and increasingly unaffordable cities like Manchester, on the other.

Ultimately, landholdings, a form of fictitious capital built, traded and renovated on the basis of the future profits to be extracted through the profitable exploitation of labour, play a contradictory but coordinating role for the spatial organisation of capital's reproduction and expansion. They also differ little from other forms of interest-bearing capital, such as government debt, the stocks and shares of enterprises, and consumer debt. The strategic conundrum which confronts Stoke-on-Trent City Council – that is, what model to adopt for the city's development – plagues state planners across the country. Henri Lefebvre's claim that urbanisation, rather than industrialisation, is now the predominant form shaping urban life, capable of modifying 'the relations of production without being sufficient to transform them', speaks to the stasis which prevails in a place like Stoke.[22] Constricted municipalities turn to private developers to create a city space fit for a more desirable coterie of professional workers without being able to attract the investment, economic dynamism and infrastructure typical of the symbiotic relationship between industrialisation and urbanisation which characterised Europe in the nineteenth and early twentieth centuries.

At one level, if we only imagine industry as a social form which forces white male factory workers into its boundless logic, then we underestimate the extent to which industries like logistics, care work, health services and retail employ multiracial, multigender labour rationalised for productive purposes, not according to the mainstream economics worldview that they produce tangible objects (though some of them do that too), but in the Marxist sense that they produce value capable of being realised as profit. In this picture, for these relatively low-paid groups of workers, the potential transformation of the city into a hub for better-earning professionals tied to jobs in richer cities poses the possibility that Stoke's rising rents, house prices and interest rates may no longer be the place for them, pushing them further out into the region's deprived urban and rural ghettos. Yet, on another level, the path towards a model of private-led urban regeneration unaffordable to the city's majority places greater pressures on the future of capitalist firms which depend on a lower cost of living, creating tensions between the demands of an impoverished service class, the strategic rationale of local employers, and city elites and real estate moguls who want to transform Stoke-on-Trent into another experiment for social cleansing, urban commodification and heritage whitewashing.

What Lefebvre refers to as the 'land-capital-labour trinity', the nexus through which all space under capitalism is produced, contested and remoulded, is by no means uniformly cogent.[23] Distinct groups of landlords, employers, and workers and tenants struggle over the terms of this trinity, and in Stoke these tensions are facing a crossroads, the chosen route of which will determine the willingness of employers to put up with higher ground rent, the city's developmental path, the ability of its citizens to escape abandonment, and the future of places like it, right across the vast urban pastures of a decaying British capitalist system. Harvey's point, that 'capital builds a physical landscape appropriate to its own condition at a particular moment in time, only to have to destroy it, usually in the course of a crisis', is precisely the situation confronting the Potteries.[24] The experience of state managers, real estate moguls, and capitalists incapable of developing a cogent, uniform strategy for the city and region is exactly the irrational, disorganised abandonment which confronts British capitalism in general, with short-term profit and rent-seeking seen as far more important than development and, ultimately, life.

For as long as the Potteries has existed, it has attracted migrants from all over the world – from the Irish and Welsh workers who dug its canal system, to the Polish and Scottish miners who joined North Staffordshire's collieries. Today, if one takes a stroll down College Road on Eid, to observe Shelton's Muslim community celebrating the conclusion of the holy month of Ramadan, or a walk through Hanley Forest Park on a warm summer afternoon, the city's rich array of cultures is visible at every turn. The arrival of Pakistani and Bangladeshi migrants in the 1970s and 1980s was followed by Eastern European migrants after the 2004 entrance of eight post-Soviet states into the European Union (EU). Just five years before, in 1999, Stoke was designated a 'dispersal city', with between 1,200 and 1,650 asylum seekers estimated to be living here. For many, the city's embrace of those from abroad has been a source of pride. But in the ailing, zero-sum political environment of twenty-first-century Stoke-on-Trent, they have also been the object of violent far-right passions and agitation.

By the early 2000s, the British National Party (BNP) was the major opposition force to the city's ruling Labour Party. In 2008, at the peak of its powers, it boasted nine councillors, majorities in a succession of local wards and the very real possibility that it might one day govern the city. The rise of Nick Griffin's BNP across the city was the result of a mixture of racialised processes on the streets and from within the state.

At the turn of the century, the city witnessed an uptick in racist violence, as recorded attacks on black and minority ethnic populations increased by 214 per cent between April and September 2001, and then by another 319 per cent following the 9/11 terror attacks on the World Trade Center. The coalescence of the BNP's rise with a set of moral panics ranged against the country's Muslim and asylum-seeker populations, primarily inaugurated by Tony Blair's New Labour, created a profoundly violent environment for ethnic minorities. As Jon Burnett has highlighted for the Institute of Race Relations, one local councillor 'actively campaigned against plans to convert a building into a hostel for asylum seekers', five Czech Roma students were forced to leave their school after a campaign of racist abuse, and asylum seekers, migrants and Muslims were routinely subjected to rounds of racist violence, including smashed windows, graffitied property and physical abuse.[25] Just a month before the milltown riots which shook Oldham, Burnley, Bradford and Leeds, with South Asian youth defending their communities against fascists, the football firm Stoke City FC – the 'Naughty Forty' – travelled to an away match against Oldham Athletic AFC and rampaged through South Asian neighbourhoods before coming back and doing the same in Stoke. When rumours spread that the BNP would organise a march through South Asian communities in the city just three months later, South Asian youth defending their neighbourhoods were brutally met with riot police.

Today, it is difficult not to feel encircled by the right. Reform UK has gained a majority on neighbouring Staffordshire County Council, transforming a council which governs over 876,000 people into a laboratory for budget cuts, gutting Special Educational Needs and Disabilities departments and dropping diversity, equity and inclusion policies. In the political ward next to mine, Birches Head and Northwood, Reform UK candidate Luke Shenton won the council by-election, accumulating more votes than all the other candidates combined. The fact that at the corner of the ward lies the Masjid Salahuddin, a local mosque which became a key target and battleground for 2024's Islamophobic pogroms, reinforces the reality of a decades-in-the-making interplay between fascist street violence and the growth of the far-right vote.

The story of 'societal decline', which Nigel Farage narrates so compellingly, posits the British nation as reeling from a 'deliberately devalued' family, broken-down communities, and a concept of national past and present thrown under the bus by the liberal left intelligentsia.[26] Against dossing woke millennials and the 'uniparty' Labour–Conservative duopoly, Reform UK is to become, in the words of Lee Anderson, a 'people's army'. This swelling multitude of older petit-bourgeois revanchists and Gen Z 'hard grafters' is fed up with high energy bills supposedly caused by net zero policies, the cost-of-living crisis and, crucially, an immigration-fuelled 'population explosion' of 10 million over twenty years, seemingly 'devaluing' British lives, infrastructure and culture.[27] Farage's declinist ruminations chime profoundly among what Ernst Bloch described as contemporary capitalism's 'non-synchronous people', those whose space and time of reproduction and exploitation sit out of step with the global rhythms of capital accumulation, even as they suffer its devastations.[28]

The slower pace of life in Stoke, shaped by its lower levels of economic activity relative to the nation's urban areas, as well as the enormous sums of land left decaying and empty, melds with the downwardly mobile, competitive impulses of a population that has been told for decades that it deserves no better than it currently has. In our city, unlike when I lived in the constantly moving London, when the prison overcrowding crisis is solved with early release, or a new wave of migration is occurring, you notice it almost instantly. As Rebecca Davies notes, talking about Portland Street, 'as soon as there's a cut to a service, you feel it instantly in this neighbourhood'.

It is precisely in this blend of factors, also conditioned by people's frustrations that they do not see what their taxes pay for except services for people they insist are undeserving of public money, that the Faragist right is able to benefit.

Sacha Hilhorst's observation that the language of the 'left behind' evades the structural reforms imposed on postindustrial towns and cities by national elites misses how the totemic image of those who are excluded from these reconfigured power relations – the often-racialised surplus populations of migrants, asylum seekers, benefit claimants, the disabled, the homeless and drug users – stands in as the conditioning form for claims of declinism, reactionary nativism and left behindness. There are some people who are left behind, and there are others who have become symbolic of falling living standards, who white workers must compete with, recriminate against and oppose. Rose Hunter, worried that the local working class might turn to Reform UK, insists that 'you blame the immigrants, you blame the refugees, you blame every fucker else except, you know, you getting up off your arse and fighting. But I never blame our class either because you've been abandoned. You've been abandoned.' The relationship between the dwindling possibility that radical change might improve the lives of the majority and the growing temptation to blame an Other isn't simply correlative. It is causal.

J. B. Priestley's observation in the 1930s that for the people of the Potteries, 'it must be either work or misery', because otherwise as a city and a region 'it has nothing to recommend it', is a reflection of both reality and the scornful attitudes with which elites and commentators have treated this city and places like it for decades.[29] In the post-1979 period, the choice between labour, on the one hand, and obsolescence or underemployment, on the other, has been stark. There are countless people, like Rebecca and those involved in the Portland Inn Project, who are successfully trying to change the city, but the conditions of possibility are constrained. As Joe

McCluskey illustrates concisely: when the 'space of the city has been forgotten', with poor transport links and long hours in a workplace distant from your home, 'that takes stuff out of people's time', this reduces the capacity of people to change the circumstances of their neighbourhoods.

While there are countless instances of people organising to transform the city for the better, we are coping today with the afterlives of a moment in British history when the powers-that-be conspired to reorganise the foundations of society and the lives of the population precisely in order to disempower radical agents who were meaningfully interrogating what a life beyond capitalism would look like. The wider story of this loss of power among the working class, of people like Rose who saw the struggles of working-class English people, not just in purely economic terms, but bound to the possibility of a better world for everyone, from black rioters resisting police racism in Toxteth, to Irish Republicans organising to end Britain's presence in the north of Ireland, is something we shall return to. For now, we ask the question, how does this crisis in population management afflicting a place like Stoke-on-Trent manifest across the nation today?

2
Disorganised Abandonment

Nothing works anymore.

Paul Nowak, Keynote Speech to
2023 Trades Union Congress

In the autumn of 2019, in the midst of the general election, I had one of the most heartbreaking experiences of my political life. Canvassing on a South London council estate, I spoke to a previous Labour voter who had supported left-wing Labour Party leader Jeremy Corbyn in 2017. He could not bring himself to do so again. He had supported Leave during the 2016 referendum on Britain's membership of the EU and felt betrayed. Furious at the courts' recent overturning of the Communication Workers Union's 97 per cent strike ballot, he identified this exercise of class power as part and parcel of the attempts by the British establishment to reject the Leave vote. He respected Corbyn, thought the problem was not him but the hostile Parliamentary Labour Party, and was wholly sympathetic to Labour's programme, particularly the parts of it which sought to transform the world of work. Even after a lengthy back and forth, we could only get this man to *reconsider* his intention to abstain. This was a trade unionist, a socialist by his own account, and a resident of Remain-voting Battersea.

A profound rupture was underway, articulated through the peculiar question of Labour's muddled approach to the EU, but expressing much deeper disentanglements between political parties and their presumed popular bases. Politics was catching up with economics, and society was processing the complicity of both Labour and the Conservatives in ruling-class assaults on the population. If, as we will see later, neoliberalism's growth years crafted an internally stratified working class that could wield equity and mortgage debt to reproduce itself, then neoliberalism's crisis years produced an indebted, downwardly mobile, low-paid proletariat, subject to far more intense forms of racialised stratification and policing, drawn to the bigger cities and forced to pay a fortune on private renting. The Tories, inaugurated in 2010 as the senior partner in a coalition with the Liberal Democrats, set about implementing a brutal austerity programme. Sold as an attempt to retract the state so as to balance the country's books, these slash-and-burn policies of fiscal prudence represented a class war from above that would leave society with a terrible, almost irreparable scar. After the organised abandonment of Thatcherism saw whole lifeworlds cataclysmically devastated and strategically undermined by an elite project of class remaking, austerity sought to craft subjects amenable to the fiscal state's agenda. But in reality it signalled a period of failed population management, jeopardising capitalism's necessary chains of social reproduction and throwing large sections of the population into a state of disorganised abandonment, felt through the lens of decline.

Under David Cameron and George Osborne, austerity measures were carefully targeted at public-service users and welfare recipients, rather than the rich or middle-class taxpayers, and the draconian cuts to local government financing overwhelmingly hurt Labour-controlled councils while leaving the Tory heartlands relatively unscathed. To note just one example among many, between 2010 and 2016 almost a billion pounds was sucked out of the North East. But austerity was not simply a budgeting exercise, it was a class project in more ways than one. Keen to dismantle the 'social state', Osborne ordained £40 billion worth of cuts, including £11 billion in welfare cuts and a two-year public sector wage freeze. The loss of 490,000 public sector jobs within four years, unemployment rates as high as 8.1 per cent in 2011, and shrinking real-terms spending on health and education were all symptoms of this administration's agenda. Yet, the Tory Chancellor also granted relief to the first £5 million of capital gains tax while decreasing corporation tax by 1 per cent each year he was in office. This project of scaling back the state, deepening the private locus of social reproduction and fattening the pockets of the wealthy also required the further disempowerment of the popular classes.

On the one hand, the 2016 Trade Union Reform Act – responding to a wave of public sector strikes over pensions, pay and conditions – raised the ballot turnout threshold to 50 per cent for successful industrial action and put time limits of six-month intervals on all disputes. On the other hand, the DWP introduced three penalty tiers for Jobseeker's Allowance claimants if they did not attend a job interview, participate in compulsory training programmes or take up a place on a course. Universal Credit merged different benefits into a digitised, reduced monthly form, geared more heavily towards incentivising the unemployed into shit, precarious work. Similarly, Work Capability Assessments put disabled or chronically ill people who were unable to work through a set of tests with no medical basis, interrogating individual 'fitness to work' through standard physical tasks such as mobility and eyesight. The Bedroom Tax, which reduced claimants' housing benefit by a sum as large as 25 per cent if their house contained one or two rooms deemed spare, was accompanied by a generalised cut to housing benefit of between

£10 and £20. Adamant that 'the welfare system ... was fundamentally broken', Osborne argued that 'benefits [are] so generous, that people found out they were better off on the dole than they were in work'.[1] This environment was sustained by a media culture in which the use of the pejorative term 'scrounger' quadrupled across broadsheets and tabloids between 2007 and 2011. In this climate, presenter Jeremy Clarkson could claim on national television that he would take striking public sector workers outside and execute them in front of their families.

The result was in many ways as intended. According to the Office for National Statistics, the austerity environment resulted in British workers spending, on average, more than forty-two hours per week at work. Large protest movements of trade unionists and students, involving hundreds of thousands of people, were nevertheless paralleled by the steady decline of trade union membership among both private and public sector workers. Even a sequence of large one-day mass strikes by public sector unions could not reverse the trend of days lost to strike action continuing to fall. A project at once fiscal, industrial and cultural, austerity was rolled out across the board.

But in many key respects, austerity did not get the goods, even on the Tories' own terms. GDP, an increasingly fetishised but hollow measurement of a nation's success, saw a meagre compound annual growth rate of 1.2 per cent, while productivity effectively flatlined over the course of the Tories' fourteen years in power. Austerity measures failed to produce a high-growth, efficient capitalist system. Shedding state capacity, increasing dole queues and fiscal tightening all rub against the key metrics that capitalists and state managers use to measure progress. What austerity does tend to prove effective at, as economic historian Clara Mattei argues, is 'insulating capitalist hierarchies from harm during ... moments of would-be social change'. And in Britain, this was no different. From the post-revolutionary years of the Great Depression and interwar fascism, to the breakdown of the neoliberal growth model, austerity has proven markedly successful at acting as a bulwark to popular rebellion, cultivating docility, hard work and individual saving among a population whose pay packet and social safety net is under assault.

Austerity, then, is class war. But more than this, it is a form of population management which aims to produce novel types of people. If the immediate aim of the British state after the 2008 financial crash was to socialise the losses of the crisis, to achieve this the state also had to socialise the people *to* loss: austerity had to fundamentally change how people think, feel and breathe throughout the ailing atmosphere of British capitalism. The increasing domination of financialisation and rentierism since 2008 has been mirrored by the population's recourse towards privatised forms of social reproduction. And people have been driven to these mechanisms by the way that austerity has gutted the state and pulverised living standards. This dynamic could be witnessed throughout the 2010s in the preponderance of rapidly rising house prices in the big cities (particularly London), a strained social housing sector with 4.5 million people on waiting lists, and a 62 per cent rise in homelessness between 2010 and 2013. In a climate that Green and Lavery claim also witnessed the longest period of falling real wages since the second industrial revolution, the reality was that workers were labouring more for less money and with less social protection. According to Tony Norfield in his book *The City*, a quarter of all households in Britain between 2010 and 2012 had net debts, while just over half had net wealth of zero to £50,000. As Adrienne Roberts has eruditely argued, in this moment of high housing costs, depressed wages and a disintegrating 'social state', workers have increasingly turned towards personal debt as a 'key means used by households to temporally – and temporarily – offset the costs of social reproduction they are not able to meet'.[2]

This spread of precariousness was also reflected in the kinds of work that were able to grow in this atrophied economic air. The post-crash years created an environment that enabled employers to exploit the workforce by cutting wages and toughening workplace conditions. In this way, austerity shifted the burden of out-of-work benefits, and the provision of public amenities like transport and postal services onto an emergent gig economy. According to the Labour Force Survey, the number of people on employment contracts with no weekly minimum hours increased from less than 200,000 in 2010 to over 900,000 in 2017. The spread of zero-hours contracts was most starkly realised in the rise of platform capitals. As journalist and author Dalia Gebrial has identified, apps such as Uber mobilised digital infrastructure to create on-demand workforces both in response to the relative surplus populations produced by the mass lay-offs of the 2008 Great Financial Crash and as a cheap fix to the austerian breakdown of state capacity in urban environments. In modern Britain, rather than the state insuring you against unemployment, JustEat provides 'flexible' work; rather than the council providing an affordable working public transport network, Uber offers dynamically priced private taxis. These two functions are two sides of the same coin. Backed by venture capital – and taking advantage of existing infrastructure, a large service sector and scalable network effects – platforms such as Uber employ a racialised working class through worker (mis)classification and algorithmic management. Labelling largely surplus migrant workers as self-employed allowed platform capitalists to drive down costs and utilise the platform app to police an already insecure workforce.

In multicultural cities and towns, the racial regime the Tories inherited from New Labour was fine-tuned and accelerated to coalesce with these new conditions of neoliberal austerity and super-exploitation. As they further disintegrated what remained of the 'social state', the Tories ensured that, in welfare, healthcare, employment and housing, austerity also created a legal and institutional basis for outsourcing everyday border surveillance. As Maya Goodfellow has documented in *Hostile Environment*, by 'stitching immigration checks into every element of people's lives', David Cameron's regime ensured that the 'threat of being fined or sentenced to jail time loomed over' all those who 'failed to carry out checks to ensure people they encountered through their work were in the country legally'.[3] Thus, the Conservatives enshrined in the dynamics of their austerity regime the increased hierarchisation of the labour market: the illusion of an illegitimate 'enemy within' ready to steal work from the indigenous labourer bolstered competition and provided a political incentive for the monitoring of racialised workers throughout everyday life. In turn, by creating an incredibly precarious racialised minority worker, the link between welfare and immigration coordinated by the British state's most repressive institutions – the DWP and the Home Office – allowed employers to drive down the conditions of workers *tout court*.

The cuts and conditionalities imposed on the country's welfare regime, resulting in a 69 per cent increase in Jobseeker's Allowance sanctions and an 84 per cent increase in Employment and Support Allowance (ESA) sanctions, produced a poorer citizenry that was more reliant on foodbanks, subject to declining living standards and more susceptible to working precarious zero-hours contract jobs. As Selina Todd has documented, between 2011 and 2012, workers employed in full-time jobs declined by 118,000, while those dependent on part-time employment increased by 86,000. These disciplinary logics, shaped by David Cameron's notion that we have had a welfare system that 'encourages the worst in people – that incites laziness, that excuses bad behaviour, that erodes self-discipline, that discourages hard work' – functioned as tools for creating a hardworking, low-paid service class.[4] Despite the punitive, austerian environment created by Cameron's Tories, the paradoxical situation of increased welfare spending and deepening public resentment towards welfare claimants grew throughout the course of the early 2010s. Spending on welfare has dramatically increased since 1979, and 7 per cent of this rise took place in the short years of that cost-cutting Conservative-led administration. Described by Chris Grover as a process of 'violent proletarianisation', the Conservative mission to punish welfare recipients threw the life chances of claimants into jeopardy. According to a 2015 study carried out by Barr et al., for every 10,000 people reassessed using ESA's Work Capability Assessment, there were an additional six deaths by suicide, 2,700 reported cases of 'mental health problems' and 7,020 prescriptions of antidepressants.[5] Importantly, austerity did not shrink welfare so much as it made people sick and created the conditions for greater welfare spending.

In 2011 alone, 131 million working days were lost to sickness-related issues, such as stress, depression or anxiety. The austerity regime may have created a legion of disciplined workers that were worse off yet less likely to rebel, but it also produced a country sicker than it had been in a long time. As the decade wore on, health professionals took to using the phrase 'Shit Life Syndrome' to describe the effects of poverty or abuse-induced disorders on their patients. Life expectancy, which had gradually increased throughout the twentieth century, slowed during the first six years of austerity. As Will Hutton documented, death rates among older people had increased so much between 2016 and 2018 that two major insurance companies, Aviva and Legal and General, were releasing hundreds of millions of pounds as reserves to pay annuities to shareholders. The reality of privatised social reproduction, turning towards insurers in the event of personal disaster, offered millionaires the opportunity for a premature payday as people lived shorter lives.

In 2008, Professor Sir Michael Marmot was asked by the then Secretary of State for Health to chair an independent review to uncover the most effective strategies for reducing health inequalities. The final *Fair Society Healthy Lives* report, published in 2010 under the Conservative–Liberal coalition, identified that there was a comprehensive link between deprivation and health, that life expectancy had slowed for many and that many lives were lived in poor health as a result of socio-economic factors. As a result, the review advocated a social metric in health and moving away from economic growth as the best measure of societal progress, while grasping that universal action on health could also improve economic indicators. The report was rejected by the new government; its recommendations were largely ignored, in no small part because the ongoing austerity mission of cutting public spending, particularly in already regionally deprived areas, was in no way congruent with the findings.

Ten years later, however, Marmot published a new review, laying out the consequences of not having followed his report's advice at the beginning of the decade. The findings of this new report were devastating. Since 2010, life expectancy had stalled for the first time in a hundred years; the more deprived the place you lived, Marmot showed, the shorter your life expectancy, especially for women. The North East and the 10 per cent most deprived neighbourhoods of London had seen the largest decreases in life expectancy. Not only did people in poorer areas spend more of their life in ill health with a lower healthy life expectancy, but since the areas they lived in also experienced the largest cuts, they were also undermined in terms of their capacity to improve the determinants of health. Across the country, but especially in the poorest parts of London and in those postindustrial areas primed for abandonment, people were dying faster and spending more of their lives in ill health than they might have done in the latter half of the twentieth century.

While there was a clear semblance of commonality between the working classes of places such as London and their counterparts in spaces of abandonment across the country's rustbelt regions, there were key differences too. The specificity of regional imbalances was a key part of the way austerity created subjects. These differences would become increasingly exploited by the political class as a way of managing the enveloping social crisis.

Standing in front of an array of cameras and media people, the then United Kingdom Independence Party (UKIP) leader Nigel Farage jubilantly celebrated. Britain had voted by 52 per cent to 48 per cent in favour of exiting the EU. The lifelong eurosceptic declared on live television that the Brexit result was a 'victory for real people, a victory for ordinary people, a victory for decent people'. Although Brexit was the product of furious debate over the future of an ailing British capitalism and its relationship to Europe, David Cameron's hubristic decision to hold a referendum was more directly a concession to Eurosceptics in his party and a growing UKIP. Just a year before, Farage's party had won 12.6 per cent of the vote in the general election. From the point at which David Cameron announced renegotiation of freedom of movement as the basis on which Britain might retain its membership of the EU, to the moment Nigel Farage claimed Leave had won the referendum 'without a single bullet being fired' – a week after the neo-Nazi murder of Jo Cox MP – the reactionary impulses of the British right were naked.

While Cameron wanted to repeat his narrow victory in the recent Scottish independence referendum, defending the interests of the British state as a neoliberal haven for multinational capital, the Leave campaign's aims were less clear. Ending free movement, implementing a points-based immigration system, ending the jurisdiction of the European Court of Justice, rolling back Brussels regulations on business and achieving independence for Britain's fisheries were all floated as the basis for the campaign. Boris Johnson's keen sense for political opportunity aside, for the venture-capitalist wing of the Brexiteers a more likely driver was the delusion of creating a 'Singapore-upon-Thames': a capitalist paradise, freed from stifling global regulations, open to the vicissitudes of laissez-faire economics and free to line the pockets of bankers while worsening conditions for workers. This referendum battle represented a process of internal dislodging which had struck the British ruling class: the strategy of moral panic over immigration and race collided with the tactic of 'Project Fear', which trumpeted the dangers that leaving the EU might pose to the status quo of British capital. However, Brexit was never simply a story of ruling-class entropy. It was also one of profound working-class discord.

The Leave campaign assembled a cross-class bloc, backed by millions of traditional Conservatives in the English South as well as a minority of the traditional political and business elite. But its victory would not have been possible were it not for the huge insurgency which swept across some of the most impoverished and downwardly mobile parts of the country. Similarly, the Remain vote was a cross-class one, encompassing huge swathes of the middle classes, the vast majority of the British elite, and a large section of workers and the poor. A remarkable outlier in twenty-first-century British electoral history, the EU referendum produced a turnout of 72 per cent. Labour's growing disconnect from and disapprobation of the parts of its working-class base it had managed to hold onto from the era of twentieth-century mass politics had exacerbated the growing rot in the heart of British democracy. Between Tony Blair's electoral landslide in 1997 and Ed Miliband's defeat in 2015, Labour had lost over 4 million votes. In a process described by James Doran as 'Pasokification', the representative binds holding people and elites together were fracturing and in need of remaking. As Peter Mair argued in *Ruling the Void*, the hollowing-out of European representative democracies was realised in declining voter turnout, heightened electoral volatility and – a reality starkly realised in Labour losing a third of its membership since the early 1980s – the breakdown of party loyalties and membership, with parties in hock to wealthy private money instead of being accountable to the members.[6] The withdrawal of parties from their mass social base and their total embrace of an elite role has represented a significant aggravation of capitalism's tendency towards democratic disenfranchisement: parties now function as government agencies, avowedly constrained by state laws and regulations. What, then, in a historical epoch noted for the sheer lack of working-class participation in elections, drove the respective proletarian turnouts behind both the Leave and Remain camps?

Class and class outcomes were obviously a huge factor. In towns and cities across the country where stable, familial life built around industry had been shattered by neoliberalism, the vote to leave the EU was majoritarian. The collapse of these settlements – from the shipbuilding hub of Hartlepool (69.6 per cent for Leave) to the mill town of Burnley (66.6 per cent for Leave) to my own Stoke-on-Trent (69.4 per cent) – was a long product of dissatisfaction at the lives and social worlds left in neoliberalism's wake. A generational process making itself felt in the punctual timeline of electoral politics, this dynamic was massively exacerbated by the effects of Cameron's austerian turn, which cut local government purse strings and demolished what remained of a local safety net in areas experiencing decline. As Tom Hazeldine noted in 'Revolt of the Rustbelt', 'The strongest Out vote in the North West came in the deprived seaside resort of Blackpool, which has suffered the greatest financial loss from government welfare cuts of any local authority district.'[7]

Blackpool provides an insightful glimpse into the character of Brexit. The Lancashire coastal town, once revered as an industrial nation's holiday resort of choice, had over the course of neoliberalism's development been deemed surplus to requirement, unable to compete with package holidays, let alone cheap flights on Ryanair or luxury apartments on Airbnb. Instead, Blackpool was developing a reputation, most searingly documented by Sarah O'Connor in the *Financial Times*, for being the embodiment of 'Shit Life Syndrome'. With the lowest life expectancy in the country, and among the highest rates of antidepressant prescriptions – over a tenth of Blackpool's population on welfare were deemed too sick to work – a town whose promenade was once known as 'The Golden Mile' now had a reputation for poor housing, crap jobs and worse health.[8] It was – and is – a warning to the working class about its life prospects under this system.

But it is also representative of the ways we think and feel about austerity, denoting a future that faces us all, as well as a symbol of capitalism's devastation of our bodies, our communities and our moral universes. As Mark Fisher argued in *Capitalist Realism*, since the miners' strike, working-class experience has been lived as 'reflexive impotence', with young people deprived of meaningful futures reduced to a kind of 'depressive hedonia', wrenching tiny pleasures out of a futile situation.[9] Consider this experience in relation to the former mining and single-industry towns, the areas where traditional class situations have been broken up and dislocated: violently uprooted by Thatcher, shredded by Blair and Brown, and reduced to ashes by Cameron and Osborne. If the depressive hedonia of the young segued into student uprisings and urban riots, then Brexit was the riot of the older, decomposed postindustrial working class of the provinces. This electoral insurgency was imbued with all the nationalist and racist anxieties which Thatcher and Blair in particular had actively sought to cultivate, and through which they had refracted historical class grievances. Given that since the 1980s very few rebellions have landed deadly blows on the system-at-large, Brexit assumed a feasibility that no genuine rupture with 'capitalist realism' had previously achieved in the period. It was a concrete offer not so much to reverse years of defeat and decomposition, but to allow people to avenge themselves both on Britain's political class *and* on its racialised outsiders. The really interesting question, then, is how to explain the peculiar object of that revolt, and so to measure its political content: if frustration at neoliberalism was part of the story here, why did it choose so apparently indirect a target as the EU, and what does that tell us about its ideological valence?

A second question, intimately bound up with the first, lies in the nature of the postwar social-democratic moment. The truth is that, beyond some notable flashpoints, Britain's working classes have rarely known class struggle to exceed the boundaries of the nation state. They are hardly unique in this respect; but if generally the nation is the modality through which classes contend with one another, the specific historical landmark represented by 1945 in Britain has more of a role to play in the Brexit referendum than is presently recognised. The postwar settlement torn apart by Thatcherism – with its lexicon of national self-sufficiency, 'Buy British', and the close intimacies it created between official, institutional class politics and economic nationalism – lingers subtly underneath the road to Brexit. The obligatory remark in the *Guardian* journalist John Harris's vox pops while traversing places like the Potteries – 'We used to make things' – speaks precisely to the loss of an industrial world built, at its best, around Keynesian national units and forms of relative affluence. This seemingly nostalgic retort to the question of 'Why leave?' is the transfigured product of the long-subdued class subjectivities shattered by Thatcher. As well as a yearning for some economic and social security, it is the reflection of a deeply rooted style of class politics bitter at the loss of a world, undoubtedly better, but still partially imagined.

The third key question posed by Brexit, then, is how the Tory right was able to marshal this complicated and contradictory structure of feeling – part nostalgia, part desire for a better world denied – into a grievance capable of being wielded for political aims. In short, the language of declinism, once mobilised by the Labour left to describe the usurping of Britain's industrial culture, has now been totally repurposed by the radical right. This transformation has a long history; its lineaments were articulated by vanguard Conservatives such as Enoch Powell, Margaret Thatcher and Keith Joseph to aggregate real material experiences of organised abandonment into a sense of national decline. The melancholic ruminations over the dilapidation of your area, the evisceration of the high street, and your basic inability to reproduce yourself, live comfortably and be happy become a neurotic fixation on the relationship between drug abuse and welfare, or between migration and crime. Farage, the latest instalment of this breed of conservative, and one of the most successful, understands better than anyone how to bend the feeling of decline that permeates everyday life into a mass politics of revanchism.

Answering these questions helps us to understand the kinds of subjects and subjectivities produced by austerity and its consequences. Thinking in these terms also helps us to consider a fourth key factor driving the Brexit vote: the influence of anti-migrant racism. According to the Ashcroft poll conducted on the day of the referendum, when asked, 33 per cent of Leave voters said that exiting the EU 'offered the best chance for the UK to regain control over immigration and its own borders'. In the same survey, 62 per cent of Leave voters thought immigration was a 'force for ill'. This spectre of the migrant as an economic, cultural or social threat has always been a feature of working-class politics, competing with proletarian internationalisms. As long as the nation is the racialised, territorial form through which economic life is organised, political struggles unravel and global conflicts are fought, there will always be a racialised outsider. But the idea of what the British nation offers has changed. By relating to class grievances routinely through the language of a limited and increasingly scarce national pool, in which immigrants infringe on the rights and living standards of the culturally conservative 'white working class', both Labour and Tory leaderships have sought to recalibrate class issues. In this distinctly austerian political language, Britain's shrivelling as a capitalist power, able and prepared to reproduce its population, is indistinguishable from the problem of too much migration undercutting wages and overstretching public resources. The oppressive conditions – insecurity, stratification and repression – that austerity visits on racialised workers themselves, for whom any embrace of racial parity must come alongside an acceptance of an exclusive and strengthened border regime, only further debilitate the construction of a proletarian internationalism encapsulating radical anti-racist class politics. In this context, the language of capitalism, class and exploitation is overrun by a cultural lexicon that absolves the structures of power of any responsibility. Satnam Virdee points out that 'socialist nationalism' has repeatedly thrived after epochal working-class defeats: the repression of mass social movements sucks the desire for solidarity into the orbit of the imagined harmony provided by the national community.[10] Brexit, then, is what happens when even the 'socialist' component of that tendency is remoulded around far more thoroughly compromised and neoliberal coordinates.

This transformation is most apparent in the flourishing of elite rationalisations of the crisis. Twenty-first-century Britain has been characterised by the breakdown of state multiculturalism and the divide in experiences of race and class between big urban areas and smaller, provincial towns and cities in the rustbelt regions; and these experiences have been politicised through a number of floating signifiers. Foremost among these signifiers is the spectre of the 'white working class', especially as it was mobilised in response to the 2011 riots. These multiracial youth uprisings against the police murder of Mark Duggan, racialised police harassment and austerity sent shockwaves of panic through the ruling class. David Cameron's claim that welfare, neglectful parents and a 'culture that glorifies violence' were responsible for the riots was given a sharper inflection by right-wing historian David Starkey, who stated to left-wing journalist Owen Jones, live on *BBC Newsnight*, that 'a substantial section of the "chavs" that you wrote about have become black. The whites have become black.' Starkey's image of a frighteningly racially composite working class epitomised Ash Sarkar's compelling claim that the riots fostered a response among political elites that sought to 'divide the working class along the lines of race and establish the category of a "white working class" whose interests would be implacably opposed to, and threatened by, calls for racial equality'.[11] Saying the usually quiet part of this normative claim unusually loudly, Starkey voiced an idea of the working class that would come to dominate popular culture in the years following the riots, and which took the place of anxieties about the undeserving white poor. Suddenly the white working class became a symbol of what Robbie Shilliam describes as the orderly and ordinary: it became media shorthand for a national story about the vast gulf opening up between the white popular classes of the rustbelt – trying hard to lift themselves out of the zero-sum character of postindustrial life – and the undeserving proletarians of the bigger cities, the source of whose fecklessness could now be located in their embrace of a nihilistic black culture that 'degenerated' the virtues of the city's older, native workers. David Goodhart, author and commissioner in the Equality and Human Rights Commission, revoiced this same spatial and racial shorthand when he claimed that the key divide cleaving Britain's working class was between 'somewheres and nowheres', implicitly setting those in the 'left behind' towns of the nation against the unplaceable refugees, migrants and their adjacent hostages in the urban melting pot.

In many respects, while the 'white working class' has a longer history than Sarkar's argument suggests, it is clear that elite attempts to think spatially about the cleavages between race and class represented an effort (especially useful to reactionaries like Farage and Starkey) to recreate what W. E. B. Du Bois referred to in the American context as the 'psychological wage'.[12] Attempting to explain enthusiasm among low-wage white workers in the American South for a system of racial segregation that enabled their own exploitation (and often their literal disfranchisement), Du Bois framed 'whiteness' as a form of psychological compensation. After the collapse of slavery, an officially sanctioned system of segregation offered poor whites access to jobs, amenities and public deference in lieu of any real economic and political power, and a higher standing than the formally freed black slaves. However, modern Britain no longer provides stable conditions for such a wage; the returns on whiteness have been diminished and refashioned in the post-crash period.

By any measure, the lives of the white working class in Britain have worsened since 1979, as have their advantages in the racialised division of labour typical of postwar social democracy. They are poorer not just in relative, but in real terms; they are less likely to go to university than at the turn of the century, more likely to work low-paid jobs and less likely to have access to a reliable safety net. The inability of elites to forge a post-2008 accumulation strategy that can absorb support from white workers – beyond relying on the legacies of cheap house prices outside of the big cities – has left in its wake only Powellite thematics without the conditions that once animated the allure of racial privilege. The right instead politicises the crisis in a reactionary direction that further shrinks the scope of the imagined whiteness of the 'white working class' by peeling poorer whites in the provinces away from the legions of multiracial workers in the bigger cities.

This dynamic finds its mirror image in the defensive nature of the working-class Remain vote, located predominantly in the bigger urban areas. It is no coincidence that the rapidly transforming cities like Manchester and London – whose relative dynamism offers their inhabitants the possibility of class mobility – gave some weight to the story that advocates of the EU told about the institution. The vision of a particular kind of cosmopolitan existence unconstrained by borders or passports, and open to a multitude of possible experiences, chimes with the official stories that London and Manchester's public institutions tell of their cities, even as property developers, landlords and untamed employers bar the possibility of its realisation for the vast majority of its inhabitants. In such places, EU membership provided a kind of psychological wage to the young urban worker.

By any measure, most Remain voters have a more progressive attitude than their Leave counterparts towards multiculturalism, climate change, feminism and many other key markers of twenty-first-century progressive politics. The two key pillars of the aloof Remain and Reform campaign, led by Jeremy Corbyn's Labour in conjunction with parts of the trade union movement, were defence of workers' rights, on the one hand, and of migration and particularly freedom of movement, on the other. There was absolutely nothing wrong with those aims in and of themselves. In the context of the toxic referendum debate they were necessary. But the campaign reflected a sad reality: to stand up against racism and the erosion of workers' rights had become synonymous with defending Britain's membership of the EU. This conjunction represented a seismic shift in both anti-racist and trade union thinking. An anti-democratic, neoliberal trading bloc – fortified at the expense of migrants and refugees and responsible for pulverising the livelihoods of workers across Southern and Eastern Europe – had been reimagined as the apparent salvation of minorities and workers.

This transformation not only signified a dulling of the horizons of socialists and anti-racists who once saw the Common Market and the state as an enemy and organiser of their oppressed existence. It exemplified the institutionalisation of anti-racism, and the defeat of working-class trade unionism. Both of these sites of radical resistance had been redirected away from mass popular action and towards a fragile dependency on the idea that the representative statist institutions of capitalist society could be relied on to defend worker and racialised minority interests. A cleavage, which opened up with the defeats of the 1970s and 1980s, found its final, farcical expression in the notion that the EU was the last hope of progressives: out of the weakness of anti-racist organisation, and the contortion of its theory, arose anti-racist Remain; out of the weakness of trade unions arose the workers' Europe.

The story of Brexit, then, is best told as one of the political decomposition of the working class as a whole (not of the left-behind white working class and the disorganised multiracial precariat). These two groups encapsulate imagined mirror images of a universal experience of abandonment. Their inverted existence meant that defending anti-racism and social rights could be convincingly pitted against sticking it to the elite, and vice versa. A profound, seemingly unbridgeable division long in the making had crashed what, as far as David Cameron was concerned, should have been a gentlemanly affair between two wings of the British bourgeoisie. Gramsci's 'active-man-in-the-mass', partitioned as he is by the contradiction between 'what unites him with all his fellow workers in the practical transformation of the real world' and what he has 'inherited from the past and uncritically absorbed', had been taken to its tipping point.[13]

One attempt to cope with this rupture in working-class coalitionism was represented by the ascendancy of socialist Jeremy Corbyn to the leadership of the Labour Party. A figure of the 1960s New Left, Corbyn combined a commitment to the democratic transformation of the British state with a humanitarian, internationalist critique of Atlantic foreign policy. The fullness of Corbyn's political agenda made it into neither his leadership bid nor his programme as leader. However, even though he stepped away from opposition to the EU and NATO, his advocacy for a 'kinder, gentler politics' revived public enthusiasm for a high-wage, social-democratic political economy and struck a chord with millions. His plain-talking disdain for the politicians' smarm and his basic humanity even gave his politics countercultural resonance. Contrary to the pattern of electoral decline and political decomposition, Corbynism inspired hundreds of thousands to join Labour to vote for him in the leadership election, and thousands to become active members. If you ventured into a Constituency Labour Party meeting between 2015 and 2019, you were likely to find a striking picture. Young graduate workers in crap jobs paying high rents, organised cheek by jowl with older, often public sector, trade unionists and retired socialists. Together these groups developed a fragile political unity against a regularly hostile party apparatus and old-guard membership.

The tension between a slick, centrist operation with dwindling political legitimacy and a fresh but inexperienced coalition of radical social democrats bled into political conflict within a year of Corbyn's successful leadership election. Following the EU referendum, Theresa May had taken over from David Cameron, who resigned in humiliation after his defeat at the hands of the Brexiteers. Labour leader Jeremy Corbyn had put down a revolt by his own parliamentarians, decisively winning a second leadership contest. The 2017 general election, which May called unexpectedly less than a year later, symbolised the zenith of the Corbyn project. Britain was embroiled in a political debate which saw the radical left rise to the challenge and foment an electoral insurgency. Corbynism's activist base was the product of the accumulated 'mental sediments' of the past forty years (from anti-war movements to student revolts), and 9 June 2017 represented the moment that a wider inchoate political coalition informed by this mix of ideas and experiences transformed into a mass electoral bloc.[14] This bloc was predicated on the fragile stymying of Labour's long electoral decline in postindustrial constituencies and the animation of the young and insecure in the big cities and university towns. On these terms, if the Brexit vote represented – as Brendan McGeever and Satnam Virdee argue – an 'articulation of a new politics of resentment underscored by structural decline and class decomposition', then Corbynism's successful transformation represented a brief, momentary process of political class remaking.[15] Typified in the mass rallies, public choruses of The White Stripes–inspired 'Oh, Jeremy Corbyn', and the #grime4corbyn phenomenon, this was a moment, à la E. P. Thompson, where large swathes of British society articulated 'the identity of their interests as between themselves ... against other men whose interests are different from (and usually opposed to) theirs'.[16] No event embodied this sense of a class present at its own making more than the wake of the Grenfell Tower incident. The product of deregulation, cuts and social neglect – and situated in a London borough shattered by a thoroughly racialised, almost-Dickensian wealth gap – the Grenfell fire provoked class revulsion across the entire country. Within days, thousands were demonstrating their anger on the streets, and the Labour leadership were boldly talking of 'social murder' and the 'requisitioning' of houses.[17] At this point, it seemed as if a new class subject was awakening on the basis of the anti-racist cultures and left social-democratic traditions which characterised Corbynism.

By 2019, however, a long process of sabotage from Corbyn's opponents within the Labour Party, parliamentary manoeuvres and wrangling over the constitutionalist horror show of implementing

Brexit had transformed the Labour leader from radical outsider into conventional politician. This absorption was compounded and amplified by the leadership's eventual u-turn to support a second referendum. Of the seats Labour lost in 2019, fifty-two were Leave-voting and only eight were Remain (six of which were in Scotland). According to a poll taken on election day, 34 per cent of voters abandoned Labour to 'get Brexit done'.[18] In spurning working-class Leave voters – and with them one of the few impactful democratic decisions older workers in particular have made in decades – Corbyn appeared 'just like the rest of them'. No wonder, then, that one of the most vociferously pro-worker, pro-poor policy programmes in history was rejected. A Labour Party that had turned its nose up at a referendum vote could no longer be deemed trustworthy enough to introduce radical social democracy. What in 2017 had looked like a tide of change, by 2019 looked like the same old Labour Party. After ten years of gruelling austerity, fortifying the intrusions and erosions of neoliberalism, with few victorious worker struggles or mass social movements to speak of, it should come as no shock that a swathe of older workers would choose the vengefully tangible option to leave the EU over a manifesto of policies which recent history had given them little reason to believe would ever materialise.

By no means an easy dilemma to solve, Brexit cut across Labour's coalition. Yet, the political decomposition of the working class into subordinate components of two warring bourgeois blocs, which could not be unified under a socialist leadership, also spoke to a deeper process of social and technical decomposition. Corbyn's compelling appeal in 2019, that whether you voted Leave or Remain, live in Mansfield or Tottenham, 'you've got high bills, rising debts, you're in insecure work, you struggle to make your wages stretch and you may be on universal credit, and forced to access food banks', was unable to join together two quite distinct experiences of abandonment, exploitation and domination.[19]

In the cities, the Thatcherite social contract had broken down under the weight of austerity, low wages and high housing costs. But this process had not quite manifested in the same way in the provincial rustbelt regions. In what was known as the 'Red Wall' – the traditionally Labour-voting constituencies in the Midlands and North of England – the devastating impacts of austerity sat alongside higher rates of owner-occupation, low interest rates and a greater reliance on individual car ownership. These were all potentially private mechanisms of insulation from the social crisis. A median-wage occupation in Mansfield, where homeownership in 2019 was as high as 69 per cent, may pay a lot less than its equivalent in the London Borough of Haringey, where owner-occupation was just 38 per cent. However, that money would go a lot further without the housing costs of a gentrified city. Encircling the slums of Stoke-on-Trent are pockets of what Duncan Weldon has called 'Barratt Britain', closed-off housing estates built by big property barons such as Barratt Homes, Persimmon or Taylor Wimpey. In the 2010s, these homes could go for £200,000 and were affordable with George Osborne's Help to Buy scheme, which required only a 5 per cent deposit, subsidising the low wages of provincial workers. Not too far from sites of extreme poverty, every rustbelt town and city contains these sites of newbuild housing, with multiple cars out front. These were pitched by housebuilding companies as ideal homes for families of four, perhaps shepherded by two parents on a modest income, a dad in sales, say, and a mother working as a beautician. For a minority of prospering workers, potentially able to escape the worst pits of a proletarian existence, the Tories' offer was not too displeasing.

What is clear now is that by late 2019, Boris Johnson's anti-parliamentary posturing had earned him the image of a radical outsider, and Corbyn had been boxed into a position of speaking, as Leo Panitch and Colin Leys put it in *Searching for Socialism*, 'not only for parliamentary decorum, of all things, but also for the rule of law itself'.[20] The most radical socialist to ever grace the Labour leadership had found himself pressured into the awkward position of reluctantly and unconvincingly articulating the decaying orthodoxies of Europhile centrists against an Oxford-bred Tory. It was this simple reality, and its relationship to broader transformations in the lives of working-class people, which brought about the death of Corbynism.

Five years later, Boris Johnson had thrown his historic majority into complete disarray by partying in Downing Street when millions were legally obliged to stay at home for months to protect themselves and their loved ones from the raging COVID-19 pandemic. Liz Truss and Kwasi Kwarteng's *Britannia Unchained* mini budget of tax cuts and Rishi Sunak's ill-fated attempt to keep the wheels on only deepened this exceptional fall from grace. The Truss regime in particular upset the Bank of England, and bond markets, unclear on how she would pay for unfunded tax cuts, triggered rocketing borrowing rates which threatened the solvency of pension funds. As well as bringing down yet another Conservative administration, this move of unbridled financial power brought to an end the decades of cheap credit which had sustained Tory domination.

Making themselves felt in the 2024 general election, the events of the 2020s have represented the pinnacle of the processes narrated in this chapter. The Tories' historic decimation at the polls, superseded by a shallow majority on the part of Keir Starmer's Labour and the breakthrough of political outsiders on both right and left, signalled the consolidation of a particular declinist structure of feeling throughout British society. The refrain, apparent in election commentary, vox pops and the like, that 'nothing worked anymore', spoke to a profound sense of abandonment among the general population, a sharp realisation that Britain was in severe decline.

But while this notion of decline is undoubtedly real, it also reflects the accumulation of a set of distinct structural processes that condition the prospects of British capitalism and the people it governs.

For starters, just as the relationship between the popular classes and their traditional forms of political representation has changed, so too has the composition of the people who rule over us. The Tories, once seen as the party of order, have been the natural political instrument for the interests of Britain's capitalist elites for well over a century. Yet these interests are by no means uniform, and in Britain a long process of their fracturing is now apparent. Capitalists – for whom 'competition now becomes a struggle between enemy brothers', as Karl Marx put it in *Capital* – have different and often competing interests.[21] For capitalism to survive, particularly in nation-state form, a 'collective capitalist' is required to put the interests of capitalism as a whole above those of the individual profiteer. The Tories have been adept at constructing the 'collective capitalist' ever since the days they transformed themselves from the party of aristocrats into the party of capital. However, the neoliberal era eroded the party's capacity to manage capitalism. Margaret Thatcher broke the labour movement, reformed the welfare state and reconstituted class rule in the interests of finance, real estate and the FTSE 100, but she also eroded the associational cultures on which her party relied – among them, the networks of elite clubs that provided the local basis for working-class identification with Toryism.[22] These changes are mirrored in transformations among the capitalist class too. The national capitalism of postimperial Britain has been superseded by a globalised capitalism, whose elite is far less internally coherent, lacks forms of collective association and is much more international in character.

State managers have always been concerned that capitalists are incapable of a long-term view, but this anxiety is even truer with regard to finance capitalists, whose day-to-day activities consist of what Thomas describes as 'fomenting … constant, chaotic change' such as 'mergers, downsizing, the immediate maximisation of shareholder value, takeovers, and restructures'.[23] The 2019 revelation that the lion's share of donors to the Conservative Party came from finance – £18 million of this from just five hedge-fund backers – only adds to the story of ruling-class short-termism. And, when one factors in the role of the state as an organiser managing, in Marx's words, 'the common affairs of the whole bourgeoisie', this short-termism has had dramatic ramifications for the capacity of the state to do precisely that.

As the late Neil Davidson has detailed, while the elected political wing of state managers has become increasingly depoliticised – as illustrated by Gordon Brown granting independence to the unelected Bank of England – so too has the unelected, non-political wing of the government – the civil service – become increasingly politicised. The corporate takeover of the civil service throughout the neoliberal period has gone hand in hand with the diminishing ideological gap between the two major parties. As a result, the state bureaucracy has become an extension of the party in power. These dynamics have implications for the relationship between the state and its subjects. The depoliticisation of the electorate and the atrophying of civil society were facts of life before 2008, but this has not been the case throughout the 2010s. The Scottish independence and Brexit referendums, Corbynism and Partygate all provide glimpses of a world that Britain's out-of-touch caste of professional politicians are ill-equipped to deal with. The Tories – and Labour for that matter – can claim the support of vanishingly few cadres able to ride out this crisis, and they can't reinvent capitalism to deal with it. The decline of the labour movement as a deep-rooted force capable of exerting its power on the state has removed from British capitalism a key social regulator capable of imposing limits on capital's unabashed commodification of all that exists.

Yet, the problem lies deeper. The disastrous impacts of austerity have produced an inadequate form of statecraft, heavily reliant on discipline and punishment, and incapable of reproducing humans, society or even amenable conditions for accumulation. As the *Financial Times* reported in an assessment of fourteen years of Conservative rule: half of children in large families live in poverty, homeownership rates have declined for all ages, capital spending on education has more than halved since 2010, household disposable income and average earnings has tailed off from postwar trends, deaths have risen sharply as a result of diabetes and heart disease, council funding has failed to match inflation (with spending per capital declining by 18 per cent), in-work poverty has risen from 29 per cent to 42 per cent and a record number of eighteen-to-twenty-four-year-olds list housing as a top-three concern. Underlying this, infrastructure has been increasingly sold off to parasitic rentiers in hock to their shareholders and uninterested in making good services for the people. Ultimately, the majority of the population increasingly live unhealthier, lonelier and poorer lives. The direction of travel of early-twentieth-century statecraft, with local government as one of the arenas in which social reformers, liberals and labour movement representatives could act to improve the health, well-being and productive powers of the population through policy initiatives, is no more. Instead, disempowered local government copes with a swelling health and social care bill alongside limited powers to raise money and less buck for your bang from the national state; the infrastructure of those vast parts of the country not subject to the vociferous impulses of gentrification has been left to rot.

Taken together, these developments provide a picture of why the contemporary British ruling class is unable to, in James C. Scott's words, see like a state.[24] Torn between its international character, and the state's much-reduced ability to manage and inability to escape the short-term thinking of financiers, rentiers and real estate, a divided, internally incoherent ruling class has forsaken any role as a rational actor. What is read by opportunist politicians as a story of declinism – a story constructed throughout the course of my grandparents' lifetime and whose plot encompassed social breakdown, crime, migration and white popular grievance – should in fact be grasped as a process of disorganised abandonment. The breakdown of the Thatcherite social contract portends a rupture in how states and classes remake and manage those they dominate. The reality of cheapened, super-exploited work, political disenfranchisement, the privatisation of space and a privatised burden of social reproduction has exacerbated the misery of everyday life for the majority since the 1970s. But this prolonged social catastrophe exploded when it confronted a state no longer capable of filling the gaps. That state now presides over exorbitant rentiers unwilling to guarantee functioning services, a society no longer able to reproduce or look after the sick and disabled, and a neoliberal settlement of low interest rates, cheap housing and easy access to credit incapable of fulfilling its side of the social bargain. In a country like Britain, people have been forced to live neoliberalism's breakdown through the process of disorganised abandonment.

As well as producing moments of political and social disintegration, this process has produced forms of disobedience and withdrawal among the popular classes. In fact, our current moment of haphazard crisis management is in large part an attempt by our rulers to rein in and reshape those parts of the population which are producing their own novel responses to the crisis of capitalism. But behind every history, lurks a prehistory.

3
The Personal Society

There ain't no need for ya,
Go straight to hell, boys …
'Straight to Hell', the Clash

The year is 1987. Stood amid a derelict engineering site, weeds growing out of the concrete, British Prime Minister Margaret Thatcher offers up a vision of retrograde futurity as an unlikely symbol of her triumph. Her 'walk in the wilderness', a photo opportunity marking the birth of the Teesside Development Corporation, is an image familiar to many of us who live in Britain's rustbelt provinces. Ironically, the promise of enterprise zones, erected on the bodies of former industrial workers as a mechanism for achieving the Conservative Party New Right's low-wage, low-tax spatial revolution, are today realised most visibly in the growth of child poverty and 'economic inactivity'. But Thatcher's vision of urban wilderness as an empty site awaiting the development that would encapsulate British capitalism's postindustrial future was in fact made realisable by her dismantling of the historically exceptional social formation known as Fordism. To grasp the roots of working-class people's abandonment in the present, and its relationship to the demise of lifeworlds and past images of what the world *could* be, we must begin with Thatcher and the world she tore apart.

Fordism, as a twentieth-century political-economic arrangement, was a strategic response to revolutionary proletarians across the Global North, participating in insurrectionary mass strikes, taking control of the factories and leading revolutions in Russia, Germany and elsewhere. Capitalists, responding to these revolutionary events, accelerated the reorganisation of the labour process already unevenly underway, breaking down each moment in the production process into minute tasks which could be monitored and timed to be carried out as efficiently as possible. By deskilling the labour process and tying wage demands to productivity, Fordism was, according to Italian Marxist Antonio Negri, a counter-revolutionary response to an insurrectionary working class. In this new paradigm, the state became the 'planner state', readjusting and regulating proletarian existence through deskilling and the mass assembly line. However, the devastation of the 1929 Great Depression signalled that ruling classes across the Global North had only half-completed their counter-revolution. The expansion of supply through these reorganised mass production industries developed within a fundamentally liberal political economy. Without the requisite growth in demand, the global economy would face a crisis of overproduction and a global depression. It was British economist John Maynard Keynes who struck at the heart of this problem from the point of view of capital.

A prosperous economy required both stability and equilibrium, and in *The General Theory of Employment, Interest and Money*, published in 1936, Keynes made the case that 'effective demand' was crucial to both. In an unstable, impoverished economy, a worker may choose to save their money; but in a healthy economy, a well-paid worker may spend and invest their money as one regulated component in a system of aggregated demand which ensured not simply stability and equilibrium, but growth too. According to Negri, Keynes saw in the unity of supply and demand the 'stabilisation of the system and thus the regulation of working-class autonomy and the "wage-unit"'.[1] The expanded techniques and capacities of state management learned during both world wars, combined with the beginning of an unprecedented growth period in the history of capitalism, paralleled the Labour Party winning a landslide majority on the promises of mass housebuilding, a National Health Service, and state-funded education, social security reforms and full employment. Under this settlement, the white male worker enjoyed greater security, a higher income and a significantly improved quality of life. Holidays, hired televisions and affordable rent were new possibilities for these workers. By the 1950s, an increasing share of the labour force worked in services, with the rise in service employment driven primarily by improvements in living standards and the concomitant rise of a new set of consumer habits connected to the popular affordability of durable goods and leisure.

Inspired by these developments, a debate arose among sociologists and cultural critics in the 1950s and 1960s over the relationship between this new consumerism and the rise of what some, notably John H. Goldthorpe et al., would call the 'affluent worker'. It was apparent that the new assembly-line employee was not representative of the traditional working class. Shorn from employment in older forms of heavy industry, and alien to the kinds of tight-knit and solidaristic bonds which characterised both urban and provincial forms of working-class communities, this modern worker, it seemed, was radically different from the proletarians who lived through the 1926 General Strike. Such workers were not yet part of a tradition of industrial militancy, worked complicated shift patterns, and sometimes lived far from the plants they worked in, driving miles to and from home and striking few social ties.

As documented in *The Affluent Worker* volumes, Goldthorpe et al. interviewed car workers in Luton in an effort to trace the subjectivity of a new class agent which was characterised less by industrial conflict and social solidarity, and more by shopfloor harmony and the single-earner male-breadwinner family model. In this ethnography, the researchers discovered that the Luton car factory workers were frustrated by the monotony and the physical and psychological stresses of the job, and dissatisfied by the pace and intensity of the production line. Nevertheless, despite their disgruntlement, they engaged in an 'instrumental collectivism' because they rightly figured it was one of the better-paid jobs in the country. As one of the Luton car workers said, 'What is it that keeps me here? Money and again money – nothing else!'[2] The Luton car workers were fully aware of the inequality of power which prevailed on the shopfloor, with one lamenting, 'We've just achieved a 15% production increase and it's all profit for the firm. Not enough production increase comes back to the workers as wages.'[3] Though, as John Westergaard has highlighted, 'It is tolerated – hardly more; and toleration goes together with acceptance of a need for everyday cooperation between management and men – for the sake of the wage packet, and essentially for that reason only.'[4] This toleration was in no small part the product of the frailty of factory workers' financial security in the period. To ensure high earnings, they worked overtime and nights on top of regular shifts, and in order to reap the benefits promised by postwar social democracy, they would often take out credit to keep up with the costly modern durables which outpaced their real wages. Throughout the late 1960s and '70s, workers would turn to large-scale industrial action on a consistent basis, even bringing down governments, in order to assert labour's autonomy on the shopfloor and keep earnings in line with inflation.

In his 1958 essay 'A Sense of Classlessness', Caribbean Marxist cultural critic Stuart Hall feared the consequences of the vastly more developed, state-centric form of capitalism he was witnessing. Wrestling with the transformative effects this new form of consumerist capital accumulation had on the lifeworlds of the working class, he paid special attention to the metamorphosis in the economic and social space of postwar proletarians. Hall feared the impact of capitalism's creative destruction on working-class subjectivity. The private home, and individual opportunity and self-improvement, had become the hallmarks of this new factory proletariat. For Hall, the emergent notion of a 'property-owning democracy', a phrase which was becoming common parlance among senior Tories, marked 'the point of deepest conflict today within the working class', as 'individual opportunity' was pitted 'against the concept of the improvement of the whole community'.[5]

After the war, large cohorts of the working masses lived in houses that had been officially condemned, declared unfit to live in as a result of wartime bombing, or were overcrowded and decrepit. Minister for Health and Housing, Aneurin Bevan, promised to build 240,000 new homes a year, and through the 1948 Housing Act committed to building council houses predicated on relative luxury, space and an indoor bathroom with toilet. The postwar Labour government, as historian Peter Malpass has argued, focused not on reform but on output. Although rent controls were introduced and local authorities prioritised as the main providers, there was 'no attempt to nationalise the failing private rented sector, nor the large house-building companies'.[6] Despite building 900,000 homes, Bevan's ministry ultimately failed to reach its target and housing remained a central concern in the 1951 general election.

Elected back into government, the Conservatives – promising the construction of a further 300,000 houses a year – would run the country for thirteen years. They would radically increase owner-occupation – from 29 per cent in 1950 to 42 per cent in 1960. Yet, in order to maintain their housebuilding commitments, they also needed to heavily rely on local authorities increasing the public housing stock. By 1961, 25 per cent of households rented their house from a local authority or public corporation, and the proportion of people renting from a private landlord had shrunk by almost half to 31 per cent in 1961. The Conservative Party succeeded in slowing down council housebuilding by removing restrictions on private housebuilding and beginning to remove rent controls in the private sector. It created a two-tiered council housing system in which councils planned who would live where, creating divisions between a richer, 'respectable' working class and its poorer counterparts. Prioritising quantity over quality, the 1956 Housing Act 'obliged local authorities to focus new housing on the residents in greatest need', building cheap housing while at the same time encouraging more affluent residents to buy their own homes.[7] The Conservative commitment to private housing found its strongest expression in Tory-run municipalities practising a version of what would come to be known as Right to Buy, with the distinct aim of converting, in the words of Hornsey MP David Gammans, 'a race of propertyless proletarians' into homeowners. While this policy would not make it into the Conservative manifesto until 1974, Labour's 1959 manifesto had already committed to reforming 'leasehold law to enable leaseholders with long leases to buy their own homes'.[8] Bevan himself had labelled owner-occupation 'an excellent thing'. Yet his fears that his vision of socially mixed housing would be superseded by class division would come true as public housing began to bear the stigma of class stratification and became entrenched in a process of 'residualisation'.

If there were trade union shop stewards at Ford Motor Company committed to keeping their hire purchase debt low and rejecting homeownership because 'they should always be in a position to take on a struggle and ... they should never be too dependent upon the company', this was an overwhelmingly minoritarian practice.[9] As we might expect, data on car workers in Luton suggests that workers who owned their homes were less likely to vote Labour. What emerged in the postwar years was, in the words of Guy Ortolano, a 'property-owning social democracy'.[10] As Stuart Hall remarked in his 1960 essay 'Supply of Demand', the consumer goods industry did not 'give us the goods: instead, it gave us a definition of the Good Life'.[11] The attainment of private homeownership became the promise of the new privatised affluence.

The developmentalist state, committed to reviving the nation's political economy by raising demand through Keynesian stimulus, had massive implications for the organisation of economic space. Local and national state planners were increasingly concerned with facilitating 'increasing affluence' and altered consumption habits, halting the 'relative stagnation of the North of England', interrogating the frailty of postwar growth, and instigating a motor car revolution which saw the number of licensed motor vehicles in Britain double from 4.5 million to 9 million between 1950 and 1960.[12] As Guy Ortolano has astutely observed, 'it became possible to understand housing construction along the lines of automobile production: as industrial projects within Fordist regimes, demanding speed of completion and economies of scale'.[13] This brief clasping of social-democratic futurity, accompanied as it was by the spread of central heating, motorisation, supermarkets, contraception and air travel, was made possible, as Christopher Harvie has documented, only by oil becoming the 'membrane connecting these revolutions'.[14]

The consumerist desires cultivated by the effects of Keynesian demand management on the private sphere, and exacerbated by the efforts of Conservative planners to spread them more thoroughly throughout everyday life, would be crucial to pulling apart popular consent for postwar social democracy. 'The serious state of unbalance', as identified by Raymond Williams in *The Long Revolution*, 'between provision for social and individual needs now exists and seems likely to increase.' There emerged a growing sense among people in the 1960s that, while social democracy had achieved a great deal, it was neither exclusively for the better, nor adequate to the needs of the population. It wasn't clear to the naked eye either, between 'the flood of new cars and the ludicrous inadequacy of our road system', for example, if the practice of planning could keep up with the vicissitudes of the market.[15] Stuart Hall, in 1960, also recognised in these transformations a developed capitalism which, on the one hand, laid the basis for a kind of communist abundance and futurity, and, on the other, reckoned with the reality that capitalism's accelerated development also militated against conditions of working-class autonomy, community and radicalism. Capitalism had created its own gravediggers on a larger scale than anything ever seen before, but the decomposition of the politically and culturally militant class agent which challenged the system through the late nineteenth and early twentieth centuries was the condition of possibility for this new social-democratic class subject.

Arriving via HMT *Empire Windrush* in 1948, migrants were excluded from the emerging benefits of this social-democratic affluence. Black workers were denied access to postwar housing reconstruction, and exploited by those landlords who would not stop them at the door with exclusionary housing practices. Searching for work during conditions of full employment, with large numbers of white workers experiencing upward mobility towards jobs that paid better, black workers plugged the gaps left by their white counterparts, encountering a labour market stratified on racialised lines which subordinated them to its lowest rungs. Overwhelmingly concentrated in manufacturing, black proletarians found employment as unskilled or semi-skilled workers in construction, textile production, shipbuilding and food manufacture. Outside of manufacturing, black workers, mostly female, were located in the emerging services of the NHS, social and private care, and transport.

Across most of these jobs, conditions were typified by unsociable hours and poor pay, and an intensely hostile and overworked environment prevailed.

The racial division of labour which emerged after 1948 saw, in the language of Stuart Hall et al., the classed living standards of black workers being conditioned by race, at the same time as white workers began to use the 'stratum beneath' them as 'material for dreams, fantasies or nightmares'.[16] And so the staging ground for the making of modern British racism lay in the transition from empire to nation state, moulded by the settlement of new migrant populations within British national borders. Prior to the Second World War, whiteness, as a colour-coded categorisation of racial supremacy, played a crucial constitutive role in the growth and hegemony of empire. As English workers were sucked into the scope of the national community, native class interests were defined as contingent on imperial hierarchies. For Alastair Bonnett in 'How the British Working Class Became White', the supreme moment of proletarian whiteness was the birth of national social democracy. The expansion of the social wage created the conditions for a renewed popular whiteness recalibrated away from the predominantly bourgeois variant of the Victorian era, and towards one reflecting qualities of ordinariness: 'it connotes lack of exceptionality, the homely virtues of quietness, tidiness, cleanness and decency'. These racial signifiers, underpinned by a social-democratic project of 'cross-class racial-national community' and born amid imperial decline, were defined against postcolonial migrants.[17] Ambalavaner Sivanandan's notion that the 'vertical integration of race' superseded the 'horizontal conflict of classes' put a lasting cast on postwar class politics, blunting the scope for popular proletarian radicalism.

By 1968, Tory politician Enoch Powell, adept at wielding moral panics in his favour, aggravated the crisis tendencies which were beginning to permanently impair postwar Fordism. His infamous

'Rivers of Blood' speech, an immediate response to the 1968 Race Relations Act, evoked the imagery of 'a nation busily engaged in heaping up its own funeral pyre', traumatised by the tragedy of the 'middle-aged, quite extraordinary working man' fearful that 'in fifteen or twenty years' time the black man will have the whip hand over the white man'. His intervention, exemplifying the ways in which processes of national decline and the diminution of proletarian affluence might be cleverly racialised, raised the possibility that the ghosts of the colonial past might threaten the orderly and ordinary independence of England. Powell posed the image of 'inner-city' Wolverhampton as the arena of this crisis. Painting an alleged picture of how, within eight years of a house being sold to a West Indian on a 'respectable street', only 'one white (a woman old-age pensioner)' remained, and 'regretfully, her white tenants moved out'. This once 'quiet street' had become a site of 'noise', 'confusion' and disorder because of its new postcolonial residents.[18]

For Powell, further propagating the racialised notion of the invaded inner city – with its substandard housing, decaying built environment and waning job opportunities – could, according to Tom Nairn, facilitate the restoration of a 'popular content to English national self-consciousness, of stirring the English "corporate imagination" into life once more', by redefining 'Englishness vis-a-vis this internal "enemy", this "foreign body" in our own streets'.[19] In London, for instance, as Robert Miles and Annie Phizacklea documented in *Labour and Racism*, between 1966 and 1974, manufacturing employment had decreased by 27 per cent and the city's population by 9.4 per cent. Shaped by declining profitability, 'white flight' and the relocation of industry, these conditions of industrial decline provided the fertile grounds on which political agents like Powell could rearticulate racism. Interviewing West Indian and English residents in Harlesden, a multicultural inner-city area in North West London, Miles and Phizacklea were struck by the 'sense of loss' among the English, who felt 'left behind in a decaying area which has been taken over by the "coloured"'. These feelings of injury were not an 'ideological "hangover" from Britain's imperial past', but instead were ways of making sense of an emergent process of deindustrialisation through this reanimated prism of racialisation.[20]

Unemployed black workers, subject to the hardships of obsolescence far earlier than their white male counterparts and inhabiting the streets of Britain's deindustrialising inner cities, became articulated as emblematic not simply of the withering of social democracy, but also of the future that lay ahead for white workers. With the effort of political actors, particularly the emerging New Right, to frame the crisis of the inner city's decline through the prism of 'muggings' and the apparent criminality of young, unemployed black men, it was possible to catch a glimpse of social democracy's competitive, zero-sum logics. Crucially, in the process of class relations being transformed by social democracy's floundering, the ways in which they were being explained by race were also undergoing profound changes. At the heart of these changes, the industrial cities which were once fleetingly the image of social-democratic optimism had now become the site of a racialised, deindustrialising entropy. This image would be used by new political actors to explain the dangers of social democracy through the prism of national declinism.

The heterogeneous class subjects that had previously taken part in over a decade of industrial insubordination – the white male Fordist car worker, the South Yorkshire miner, the part-time female clothesmaker and the black foundry worker – had not simply fought for higher wages. They had fought for greater control over the shopfloor, contested the employers' right to manage, brought down governments, defended old proletarian lifeworlds from ruin and struggled for the right to be free as women, as black people and, crucially, as human beings. Their power to do so had often been enabled by what Michał Kalecki has described as the 'political aspects' of full employment. With the threat of the sack lacking its usual impact in the absence of mass dole queues, workers in that time exercised a degree of power unseen outside of periods of revolutionary instability.

In contrast, in the throes of deindustrialisation and the concomitant rise in unemployment, workers in the 1970s who sold their labour in the factories gradually confronted a harsh reality. Faced with the possibility of visiting the Labour Exchange on a Monday morning instead of working on the line, these workers would become entrenched in Joshua Clover's 'affirmation trap'. Rather than demanding greater free time, or democratic worker control, industrial employees were faced by the late 1970s with a situation in which, to fight for their own survival, they would have to bind themselves to their boss and fight for the conditions of the capitalist firm's survival itself. To avoid poverty and obsolescence, they would now have to affirm their status as a worker and their dependency on the employer, removing the conditions of their previous militancy in the process.

Tying workers to the domination and exploitation of the factory floor, national social democracy rearticulated colonial and patriarchal relations of power through such timeworn concepts as skill and productivity. The Endnotes collective's notion of 'unity-in-separation', in which the social unification of some on the factory floor becomes the basis for their integration into capitalist production and their atomisation outside of the workplace, was the key hurdle any genuine effort at proletarian autonomy would have to leap over. The reality of high wages, access to television, home-ownership and holidays by the sea may have been good enough to make the myth of the 'collective worker' believable. Yet the actuality of driving to work every day, undertaking backbreaking labour, working overtime to pay off hire purchase debts and mortgages, and living a life of relative privatised affluence were, unsurprisingly, no consolation. The metamorphosis of the passions and sentiments evident during the 1926 General Strike and the Great Depression into what Guy Ortolano has described as a 'property-owning social democracy' signified a breakthrough in the history of capitalism.[21] For the first time, on a mass scale, proletarians became working-class propertarians, having something to lose other than their chains. Both public and private sector workers, from the 1968–75 strike wave to the Winter of Discontent at the end of the 1970s, were undermined by the growing obsolescence of deindustrialisation, absorbed into partnership agreements as a result of their reduced bargaining power and divided by James Callaghan's fiscal tightening of the social-democratic state, foreshadowing Thatcher's efforts to pit those who were dependent on the state and those who weren't against one another.

Thatcher's oft-quoted remark 'Economics are the method; the object is to change the heart and soul' offers us a glimpse into the heart of Thatcherism. The project of overcoming high inflation, a sclerotic social democracy, bountiful social wages and a powerful working class required the creation of a new moral economy. To realise this, the Tories had to pull the rug from underneath the lifeworlds of insurgent, emancipatory subjects. In doing so, they relied on a vision, laid out by the early New Right, of right-wing economics as a project of reactionary social engineering, concerned with people's souls as much as their incomes. A decade prior to Thatcher's electoral victory, figures such as Keith Joseph were developing on the *Weltanschauung* of Powellism, founding the Centre for Policy Studies and elaborating a new vision of monetarist eugenics geared towards disassembling national social democracy and the social agents it bred.

In 1974, during the last months of Edward Heath's Conservative government, Joseph spoke to a Birmingham audience asking his allies why they speak to the public as 'economic men' and not as 'whole men' concerned with the state of the nation, the welfare of their children and the health of the body politic. Urging Conservatism to revive the family as the foundation of the nation, Joseph questioned the morality of a 'permissive society' which ceded the determination of the private citizen to a state which encroaches on individualism and engineers social decline through delinquency, crime and teenage pregnancy. Fearful that the 'balance of our population, our human stock' was under threat from the rise of young and single working-class mothers, Joseph insisted that Toryism should embrace Freud's reminder that 'repression of instincts is the price we pay for civilisation'.[22] In this assessment, the Fordist paradigm had unleashed a tidal wave of distinctly primal social evils: the expansion of sexual liberalism enabled the rise of divorce and the declining birthrate; postwar immigration birthed the spectre of 'muggings', Black Power and the racialised decline of the inner city; and the spread of political and cultural permissiveness into the workplace accelerated industrial rebellion and the quest for greater freedoms on the factory floor. Joseph's weaponisation of a set of cogent moral panics signified a burgeoning New Right seeking to redefine British culture. But to be successful, as Thatcher and her allies were keenly aware, the industrial vanguard of this new permissiveness would need to be not only morally and politically condemned, but ultimately vanquished.

After Thatcher's election as Conservative leader in 1975, the political institutions around her spentthe next four years preparing for power. Selsdon Group founder Nicholas Ridley, for example, produced a report in 1977 detailing one potential approach for government. Committed to the privatisation of all nationalised industries and the conversion of the people into 'customers', Ridley outlined a three-pronged plan. First, nationalised firms would be subject to conditions and sanctions in the event of failure, company boards would be reorganised to marginalise labour representatives, state interference would be curtailed, state buyouts made a thing of the past, and wage settlements made conditional on productivity and profitability. Second, companies would be sold to private owners, broken up and their public status legislated against. And last, preparations would be made for a set of piecemeal, strategic confrontations with the most ardent defenders of the nationalised firms: the trade unions. Underlying this plan was a realisation that an embattled Tory government would have to bide its time. A political long game was required to retool and reform a police force fit to face down pickets, to remove welfare benefits for strikers, to grant concessions to 'vulnerable industries' from which the economy was least insulated and to stock enough energy – most importantly coal – for prolonged confrontations.[23]

Voted into office in 1979, Thatcher was immediately faced with a global economic slump as a result of the Iranian revolution and the subsequent drop in oil production. Britain's industrial economy – wracked with 13 per cent inflation, well over a million unemployed and a breakdown in the corporatist model of state-mediated class compromise – was acutely vulnerable to worldwide shocks. The manufacturing overcapacity and deindustrialisation which had plagued Britain throughout the 1970s grew over the next decade, and the country fell behind ascendant industrial powerhouses such as Germany and Japan. Unlike Callaghan's Labour, the New Right was not constrained by the need to meld monetarist economic policy with the structures and parameters of Keynesian social democracy. Rather, the Thatcherites sought to deconstruct the architecture of the postwar settlement, tightening the money supply, raising interest rates and slashing public expenditure. This had the dramatic effect of the pound appreciating and the exchange rate being driven up, forcing companies to downsize and sack employees in the process.

For every ten manufacturing jobs in 1971, only seven remained ten years later. According to Jack Robertson, 53 per cent of the strikes which rocked Britain in the militant period before 1980 were carried out by just 4 per cent of union members. The industries which had hired these militant workers – metal manufacturing, textiles, clothing and footwear production, docking, shipbuilding, coal mining and vehicle manufacturing – were the sites of employment most damaged by the 1981 recession. As Huw Beynon has detailed in *The Collapse of Manufacturing*, industrial regions like the West Midlands underwent a devastating process of lay-offs, losing 1,000 jobs a day at the height of Thatcherite deindustrialisation.

In this harsh environment, the elasticity and power workers had taken advantage of throughout the era of full employment came crashing down under the weight of 3.5 million unemployed by 1983. Conditions of mass redundancy and falling real wages restricted workers' appetite for defensive economic struggles; or worse, it bound workers to their employers as a protective move against their own obsolescence. Throughout the following years, workers would suffer decisive defeats on the railways, in education, among TV-AM technicians, in printing, on P&O ferries and most notably in the coal mines. On the one hand, rapidly declining profit rates and a slump in productive output petrified industrial employers and provoked protests from the Confederation of British Industry. On the other hand, faced with recession, employers could raise the threat of the firm's economic viability against the demands of labour, a scare tactic that was weaponised effectively because, in the words of Simon Joyce, 'it is true: if the company doesn't make a profit, it *will* go out of business'.[24] The exceptional epoch of postwar social democracy, with its historic rates of economic growth, was coming to an end, erasing the structural power and combativeness of militant workers with it.

Vehicle manufacturer British Leyland (BL), under the stewardship of Michael Edwardes, waged an employer's offensive under the cover of recession. The image of Derek 'Red Robbo' Robinson leading a picket line of striking workers in 1977, defending their right to work, foreshadowed the Communist Party activists' own victimisation in 1979, unsupported by the majority of the BL workforce. The management were intent on taking advantage of this precarious industrial environment. 'Workers' participation' was quickly transformed into the erosion of national collective bargaining, and the return of 'individual and plant-level bargaining, performance-related pay and unilateral imposition of new, less favourable labour contracts'.[25] Between 1972 and 1982, the BL workforce was halved from 164,000 to 80,000. Motivated by organisational survival, a decade of disputes at BL evidenced the extent to which union structures were forced into simply protecting themselves. This pragmatic preservationism would come at a great cost. Unemployment levels among manual workers were more than double those of the rest of the workforce. Older workers suffered the most, and whole regions witnessed the economic sinews of their lifeworlds disintegrate before them. Beatrix Campbell captured the situation for Northern and Midlands workers under Thatcher: 'On whole housing estates half the population are on the dole, permanently hibernating at home while children go to school.'[26]

The fear of obsolescence, mediated by the prospect of destitution and the unravelling of workers' legal rights, permeated right through the proletarian population. Ron Todd, chief union negotiator at Ford, told the *Financial Times*, 'We've got three million on the dole, and another 23 million scared to death.'[27] Another factory convenor described the 'terrified' atmosphere among union members; 'hundreds of pairs of eyes' were fixed on him when he left the negotiating room, many petrified that the firm was 'going to close'. As the General Operations Manager at Ford's Halewood plant had made clear, Thatcher had 'contributed to the workers' realisation that if they don't do a solid day's work they're out because the government won't save them'.[28] In fact, even this straight-talking account of government indifference underestimates things. The 1979 Conservative election manifesto wanted to reform manufacturing production, free up profitability and productivity, and diminish both state and trade union influence. The plummeting of Britain's industrial economy – and the unemployment it brought – was not just a tolerated consequence but a deliberate product of Thatcherism's belligerent class politics, its unbridled willingness to dismantle working-class collectivism. This was class war not just in the form of an industrial dispute, but as a calculated attempt to destroy the very way that Britain's industrial working class reproduced its lifeworld.

One group of workers who typified exactly the kind of society that the British New Right wanted to destroy were the miners. Disproportionately affected by deindustrialisation and Britain's transition to an oil economy, the miners were at the sharp end of Thatcher's class war from above. But the mineworkers were uneven in their political composition: the 'little Moscow' of South Wales and the Scargill-led radicalism of the South Yorkshire miners, absolutely central to the demise of Edward Heath, did not necessarily reflect the politics of the whole workforce. The north Nottinghamshire coalfield was the 'jewel in the crown' of the National Coal Board (NCB). Its uniquely geologically prosperous location, as Jay Emery has detailed, proved it to be the most productive, most profitable and, consequently, most shielded from international competition. Its relative protection from deindustrialisation (Nottinghamshire mines lost only 778 jobs throughout the 1960s and 1970s) imbued the north Nottinghamshire miners with a sense of security and insulation from the woes of the national industry that ultimately resulted in most of the workforce refusing strike action when the miners' confrontation with Margaret Thatcher began in 1984.

As well as being internally divided, this vanguard battalion of the labour movement faced a government which had spent five years preparing for battle. Having almost doubled coal stocks to guard against the event of strike action, increased imports and extended dual firing at coal stations, Thatcher went to war with the miners in 1984 on the back of a second election victory, using her renewed political mandate to appoint renowned union-buster Ian MacGregor as the head of the NCB. MacGregor quickly announced the closure of twenty collieries and the loss of 20,000 jobs, commencing a year-long dispute. Facing an existential battle, the National Union of Mineworkers (NUM) was inhibited by divisions within the workforce. Fearful the union could not pull off a majority in a national vote, regional ballots were rolled out, with the Nottinghamshire, Lancashire and Derbyshire miners voting against strike action. Similarly, the timing of the strike, launched in the spring of 1984, meant that it had less economic impact than it would have if it were initiated in the autumn. The endurance of the Thatcher regime, its ban on secondary picketing in support of the miners, its reduction of social security benefits for strikers, and the mobilisation of a spectacularly repressive and mobile police force all served to marginalise a group of workers who had been thrown to the wolves by their employers and abandoned by Labour.

Despite its defeat – an existential one insofar as the future of the labour movement was concerned – the miners' strike showed flashes of the alternative moral economy which the New Right sought to dismantle. The miners' wives and the women of the pits, people like Rose Hunter, constructed a culture of social solidarity and popular welfare in defence of their communities, organising public kitchens and food distribution centres. And as Diarmaid Kelliher documents in *Making Cultures of Solidarity*, the experience of deindustrialisation in London, combined with the NUM's recent support for the Grunwick strike in the north west of the capital, created a situation in which the city mobilised heavily in support of the strike. To take one example, Staffordshire miners attended Notting Hill Carnival during the strike, 'where they had stalls, a float, and distributed badges that read "Black People Support the Miners", and "Oppose Police Violence"'.[29]

These connections speak to more than heroic acts of solidarity across distinct communities. Notwithstanding the Conservative ambition to break up the radicalising subjects of the postwar period and revive a racially sanitised family institution from the afflictions of worklessness and cultural pathology, the project of Thatcherism threw millions of white workers into circumstances of industrial obsolescence eerily similar to those first experienced by black proletarians. In precisely the period when work was less likely to become the site of a political unity between racialised minority workers and their white counterparts, shared processes of obsolescence, state repression and learning from one another's experiences of oppression created space for a limited unity between groups of workers who occupied distinct positions in the labour hierarchy of postwar social democracy.

The New Right were acutely aware of these processes. In the 1979 election campaign, they released a Saatchi and Saatchi–designed poster depicting a long dole queue, stating: 'Labour isn't working.' Playing up the centrality of work to realising the benefits of Keynesianism, the Tories were reinforcing the division between productive, disciplined workers and unproductive, parasitic paupers, while simultaneously demonstrating that the current state of affairs might visit on white workers the same destitute destiny as many of their black peers. Ultimately, the message was that the social-democratic high-wage economy was no longer bringing home the bacon. Instead, it was restricting the economic freedom of the British citizen. Benefiting from an enormous windfall from the sale of North Sea oil, the Conservatives introduced means-tested benefits as a staple of Thatcherite statecraft supplementing monetarism and anti–trade union legal reform in the quest to reduce workers' bargaining power, levying income tax on welfare and reducing benefit payments in the process.

David Young, Secretary of State for Employment, constructed a regime of conditionalities, ensuring that claimants were 'available to work' and forced to undergo formal interviews in order to undergo job training. Jim Tomlinson's contribution in *A Neoliberal Age?* has rightly stressed how, as later Chancellor of the Exchequer, Nigel Lawson concentrated on 'the rediscovery of the enterprise culture' through the removal of any 'rigidities and distortions' in the labour market.[30] Lawson was especially eager to reproduce US patterns by increasing the number of part-time and casual jobs in an expanding service sector. The spread of low-paying jobs in education, health, social care and services was accompanied by a substantive rise in state spending on welfare. In short: while Thatcher reformed the welfare state and the social wage to contravene proletarian power, she massively increased expenditure on conditional welfare to cope both with rising unemployment and with deliberately aided changes in the structure of employment. The image of obsolescent wilderness at the beginning of this chapter was the condition of possibility for the insecure moral economy the New Right wanted to birth.

This apparent contradiction between Thatcherite ideology and practice by no means made life easier for proletarians. In 1986, 1.3 million people had been out of work for more than one year and 800,000 for more than two. While the young were the target of the state's efforts to engineer entrepreneurialism and subsidise employment through vehicles such as the markedly unsuccessful Enterprise Allowance Scheme, the old were organised for abandonment. With the economy shifting towards service-based, often feminised, forms of labour, older workers became a less appealing prospect for employers. The world of 'front door socialism' communicated by one trade unionist as 'politics first, family second', beginning when he 'shut the front door' and ending when he 'came home', relying on his wife as an 'emotional sponge', had been overturned, in the words of Linda McDowell, by 'redundant masculinities'.[31] While female workers were substantially affected by deindustrialisation too, the gendered division of labour in Britain's transforming political economy resulted in a greater number of single-earner, female-led households. As Beatrix Campbell demonstrated, this 'evoked a sense of mass martyrdom, a kind of death' among unemployed men, in no small part because their exclusion from work also meant their ejection from the social activity which underpinned their masculinity, their sense of self, depriving them of 'their route to masculine class consciousness and class strength'.[32]

Under Thatcher's initial pension reforms, older ex-workers saw their pensions decline to just 14 per cent of average earnings as they became indexed to prices rather than earnings, and the unemployed could boast an existence barely different from their forebears in the 1930s. As Ian Jack noted at the time, the unemployed in the 1980s could afford a telephone, a washing machine and a television, but like their grandparents before them, fresh fruit and the butchers were out, while bread, Clothing Clubs, corned beef and little extra expenditure were in. The conversion of the industrial world of work, labour clubs and union nodes into mass unemployment disrupted their social life, emptied their time of purpose and fundamentally made them 'feel unmanned'.[33]

The government could play down the extent of unemployment, reclassifying older workers as 'in early retirement', or as groups of ex-workers incentivised to chase heftier sickness benefits over squeezed unemployment payments, exemplified as 'long-term sick'. The economic activity rates among males aged between sixty and sixty-five plummeted from 83 per cent in 1971 to 55 per cent in 1987, with only a fraction of the remaining 45 per cent counting as unemployed. The prevalence of industrial injury among the laid-off population also enlarged the number of people on invalidity and sickness benefit, which doubled between 1980 and 1993 to 2 million. This increase was compounded by the growth in interpersonal adult care, with one in every seven adults providing regular care of around twenty hours to sick, disabled or elderly people. But such reclassifications did not undermine the scale of the transformation underway in British society. The sympathetic figure of the unemployed worker once symbolised a historical moment that the nation would never return to. But, having destroyed the political compact and ways of life that sustained the Keynesian commitment to full employment, the New Right was able to rearticulate this archetypal figure into a critical symbolic part of their successful mission to spring the 'affirmation trap' and decisively shift the dial on Britain's political culture. Thatcher's story in her memoir, *The Path to Power*, directly connected the rise in crime, divorce rates and welfare dependency with growing unemployment and the breakdown of the family. This was the construction of a cultural explanation for the types of unappealing subjectivities produced by social democracy's disintegration.

If Thatcherism was a project cultivating populations in its own image, no cohort of the population epitomised the challenges of this reactionary impulse more than the 'folk devil' of Britain's racialised minority population. Mass unemployment had the effect of significantly curtailing the resources, structure and capacity for political action among working-class men and women of all ethnicities. The latter worked harder at their jobs and their partners were not picking up the slack at home, while bus fares and pints at political meetings cost money the former simply did not have. Yet, these phenomena did not just have a deeper impact on the country's racialised minority communities; they were also a section of the population that had experienced the brutal, impoverishing grind of obsolescence far in advance of the country's largely white industrial battalions. The severity of the treatment faced by unemployed black youth at the hands of employers and state agents sparked a widespread street uprising that would have a disproportionate impact on the relationship between race, class and space.

By 1985, unemployment among white males averaged 11 per cent, compared with 15 per cent for Indians, 24 per cent for West Indians and 28 per cent for Pakistanis.[34] This mass of the racialised unemployed also confronted a growing escalation of repressive policing. The 'sus' laws, derived from new powers the Thatcher government had inserted into the Vagrancy Act 1824, provided the police with a pretext to establish 'reasonable suspicion' that a crime had been committed. This became the basis for the criminalisation of black youth for simply being black and being out on the street. Peter Bleksley, a Metropolitan Police officer in 1981, later claimed that 'sus' was used 'to basically "fit up" and brutalise people that we didn't like'. In 1980, Simon Peplow documents that 1,469 people – black and white – were arrested under '"sus" throughout London: equivalent to only one-third of stops of black people in Brixton alone'.[35] The racialised parameters of crisis Britain had produced a culture of racialised violence. In 1981, the year of the riots and arguably one of its triggers, thirteen black youth died in a racially motivated arson attack in London's New Cross.

The first spate of riots, kicked off by a brutal plainclothes police operation labelled 'Swamp 81', were, in the words of Darcus Howe, of 'insurrectionary proportions', encompassing the multiracial urban poor across over thirty-five towns and cities including Liverpool, Manchester, Nottingham, Leeds and Birmingham.[36] Within four years, another round of riots had engulfed Brixton, Toxteth, Peckham and Tottenham. Erupting in response to acts of police harassment, or worse, murder, these more short-lived rebellions marked the beginning of the end for this period of black radicalism.

The novel experience, conveyed by a teacher and trade unionist, of chucking 'all the history we were doing out of the window' and teaching 'the history of rioting for a week', while a class of 'most interested' kids picked 'glass out of each others heads', was coming to an end.[37]

The riots, spawning organisations such as the Broadwater Farm estate's Movement for Civil Rights and Justice, had politicised the question of unemployment far more effectively than the 1981 People's March for Jobs, which was isolated by both the Labour Party and the trade union movement. In its manifesto, the movement could raise its community opposition to capitalism, highlighting rising unemployment as a product of an 'international division of labour' which strips industry from countries with 'strong trade unions and organised labour movements to places where there is no democratic rule and revolts are crushed with machine guns'. These conditions of racialised obsolescence mirrored forms of exclusion and precarity elsewhere. As the experience of Oldham's Kashmiri and Pakistani mill workers epitomised, racism continued to work through practices of labour market – and labour movement – exclusion. South Asian mill workers were concentrated, as Virinder S. Kalra has detailed, on the night shift, in both a declining industry and an occupation vulnerable to redundancy. If these workers were fortunate enough to hold onto their jobs through the course of multiple recessions, they could then be faced with the degrading effects of work on their bodies, ruining their knees, putting them on sick pay, but also leaving them excluded from what remained of the social life of the white labour movement, with its pubs, working men's clubs, and institutions of health and welfare.

The Movement for Civil Rights and Justice, based in Tottenham, would articulate this problematic in its 1987 manifesto, demanding 'Success through caring': organising for jobs and better employment opportunities, renovations to housing and the estate, training and educational resources, and better services. It did this in opposition to the managed decline of their area which, much like the Portland Street estate discussed in Chapter One, had been etched into the 'theatre of politics' by the New Right in characteristically racialised terms, with the Metropolitan Police and the press depicting a troubled estate symbolising the nation's social decline. As this process of class decomposition pressed on, some rare strongholds of enduring radicalism, such as Broadwater Farm, kept the fire alive, but an emerging phenomenon of incorporation, blunting black anticapitalism and forging a black accommodation to the status quo, would quell it further.

In the wake of the 1980–1 riots, the Scarman report was published. This highlighted the need to address racial inequalities, but did so in the language of 'equal opportunities'. Paul Gilroy, in 'The End of Anti-Racism', described a context in which local authorities created the conditions for 'competition between different political forces over which of them is going to take immediate priority'.[38] The postindustrial city, rationalised by the New Right as a space of hopelessness, decline and multiculturalism gone awry, epitomised Thatcherism's successful reframing of opponents the New Right once acknowledged as worthy enemies. The spread of municipal radicalisms like Ken Livingstone's Greater London Council (GLC) saw the New Left attempt to deliver democratic socialist solutions to the breakdown of postwar Keynesianism, resisting the tide of Thatcherism, opening local government to feminist, LGBT and anti-racist self-organisation, and experimenting with alternative worker politics.

But this shift away from workplace and street politics struck an awkward chord for a succession of waning social movements. Late-1970s Britain had witnessed electrifying displays of anti-racist and interclass solidarity, best typified by the strikes by Asian women workers at the Grunwick processing plant and the countercultural Rock Against Racism movement. By the late 1980s, anti-racism had undergone a process of institutionalisation. The convergence of the 1980s riots, and GLC anti-racism, produced the conditions which cut anti-racism off from its long-fought-for, and rocky, relationship to emancipatory politics. From the far left to the Asian Youth Movements, coteries of younger militants, informed by a commitment to proletarian internationalism, had done their utmost to intertwine anti-racism and class struggle throughout the preceding decades. The 1980s, however, produced a different layer of racialised *insiders*.

The government responded to these insurrections by introducing inter-ethnic competition for funding, which contributed to the broader disorganisation of black militancy. What anti-racist activists saw as efforts to build strata of collaborative interlocutors committed to undermining rebellion, began to succeed in a context of social movement disintegration. As Sivanandan argued in *Communities of Resistance*, the 'self-reliance and community cohesion' that had been constructed around 'political blackness' in the 1960s and 1970s was unravelled by the state through the 'emergence of an Afro-Caribbean managerial class in the race relations industry', seeking to 'deepen ethnic differences and foster ethnic rivalry' through the parcellised distribution of community funding and grants.[39]

Despite its strengths, the GLC was also the object of anti-racist criticism. The growth in local government employment of minorities and the existence of a bureaucratic layer within the state overseeing the institutionalisation of anti-racist politics led to the identification of equality with 'efficiency and good management practice', ensuring that 'policy questions dominate political ones and anti-racism emerges from the production of general blueprints which can be universally applied'.[40] The absorption by local state bureaucracies of political demands that had first emerged from grassroots politics furthered the bifurcation of anti-racist practice.

Even in the combative efforts of Livingstone's GLC, the 'council becomes the primary site of anti-racist struggle' where, according to Gilroy in *There Ain't No Black in the Union Jack*, 'the general task of advancing anti-racism is thereby collapsed into the specific strategic priorities of the GLC, a model which regardless of its in-house ineffectiveness, is not universally applicable to anti-racist politics in non-institutional settings'.[41] As a product of defeat, anti-racism shifted from seeing the state as an enemy, to seeing it as a vehicle for mitigating racism through a parcellised distribution of 'equal opportunities'. Race was detached from class, and anti-racism was de-radicalised as the state usurped the role of protest, riots and strikes. As Kieran Connell has demonstrated in *Black Handsworth*, 'even at the level of the local ... ideas about an encompassing black political colour weakened'. The integration of community leaders into the state was one thing, but local organisers confronting the gamut of joblessness, poor housing and poverty were forced to 'perform the role of the dedicated social worker', appealing to the state on identitarian grounds for resources.[42] The condition of possibility for this disassembling of black radicalism was the spatial regime inaugurated by Thatcherism, as disastrous for the inner city as it was for the small industrial town and pit village.

If, as Neil Brenner has argued, the postwar era involved a sort of 'spatial Keynesianism' – whereby the nation state sought to mitigate uneven geographical development through the planned construction of new urban and suburban networks – spatial Thatcherism was quite different. For the New Right, uneven development became a necessary precondition for reasserting capitalist power. This emerging settlement rose through the confluence of three factors: the decline and restructuring of mass production industries, the rise of flexible production systems, and the globalisation and integration of European economic space. This new growth-oriented and competitiveness-driven approach to urban governance resulted in sharpened uneven development as strategic locations and cities became the predominant sites for transnational capital investment.[43]

Accelerated growth in the English South went hand in hand with industrial decline in the Midlands, South Wales and the North. In Liverpool, a historic dock city, the decimation of industry, from the Kirkby Manufacturing and Engineering site to the Love Lane Tate & Lyle factory, was deeply entangled not just with Thatcherism but with a broader economic reorganisation begun under former Labour prime minister James Callaghan. In 1981, a Right to Work campaign leaflet could demand that the 'murder of Merseyside' be stopped, while the Socialist Research Group accurately described the city as the 'Bermuda Triangle of British capitalism'.[44] This uneven economic geography would become part and parcel of twenty-first-century Britain, a capital of global financial and rentier speculation dramatically diverging from other regions and nations.

One of the ways in which the government helped create this regime was through the implementation of enterprise zones geared towards delivering Britain's industrial population from its 'urban wilderness'. The organised abandonment created by recession, deindustrialisation and the New Right's class war had devastated the physical space of proletarian Britain, extending dole queues, emptying warehouses and filling the streets with the homeless. Mainstreamed by Geoffrey Howe prior to his appointment as Thatcher's Chancellor of the Exchequer, enterprise zones were first initiated in the 1980 budget, with the London Docklands, Liverpool, Newcastle, Trafford and ten other zones being formed in the first three years of the Thatcher government. Howe argued that Britain's cities faced increased social tension between obsolescent populations mired in a space devoid of growth. These areas had been 'blitzed' by top-down state planning, and the challenge these sites of 'urban wilderness' posed to revival necessitated the opening-up of enterprise zones.

As Sam Wetherell has outlined in his essay 'Freedom Planned: Enterprise Zones and Urban Non-Planning in Post-War Britain', the creation of enterprise zones – grafted onto industrial, manufacturing spaces of old such as the Isle of Dogs – granted businesses a series of incentives, including exemption from the Development Land Tax, negligible regulation and scrutiny, 100 per cent capital allowances for industrial or commercial buildings and a streamlined planning process. Keith Joseph, in a memo to Margaret Thatcher, set out a vanguardist vision of these zones as 'demonstration areas' in advance of a more comprehensive legislative revolution, 'where conditions more encouraging to enterprise might be established – to show what would then result'. These experiments, ultimately concerned with what David Harvey has described as the transition from urban managerialism to urban entrepreneurialism, sought to 'lure highly mobile and flexible production, financial, and consumption flows into its space'.[45]

The formation of the London Docklands Development Corporation (LDDC) in 1981, marketed as 'Wall Street on water', was deemed to be a beacon of unshackled economic growth. Hit by a wave of depopulation in the preceding ten years, the Isle of Dogs had seen unemployment 6 per cent above the national average and 86 per cent of its residents were council tenants. After six years of state-mandated 'enterprise', however, the LDDC could hardly boast success. By 1986/7, the borough unemployment rate was 13 per cent higher than the London average; jobs had grown in banking and finance, as well as in the distribution, hotel and catering sectors, but 11,000 jobs had been lost in manufacturing, and the number of the total workforce who lived in Docklands in 1981 had declined from 32 per cent to 21 per cent. This once-crucial industrial artery had been transformed into a privately owned, service-dominated zone of abundant private accumulation. Before Canary Wharf had even been approved, capital was taking advantage of the effects of containerisation, relocating businesses into the area as fuel for growth, cleansing the place of its historical populations and converting its council tenant population into a mixed-tenure citizenry encompassing a far larger homeowning cohort.[46]

East End socialist and doctor Dave Widgery saw only 'a wonderful folly to the excesses of Thatcherism', a vehicle for the gentrification of old London which pitted the flash icons of financial capitalism next to the ruins of a bygone age, while property developers and landowners made it rain.[47] Even so, this classed radicalism was by no means how the area's transformation was read by the Isle of Dogs' inhabitants. While the image of dockworkers downing tools in support of Enoch Powell looms large in the national memory, less remembered is a general pattern of racist pogromist violence against minorities in the East End which culminated in the electoral success of the far-right BNP in the early 1990s: BNP member Derek Beackon was elected to Tower Hamlets Council in 1993 and achieved 14 per cent of the local election vote a year later in Newham. The party achieved this by constructing 'a "common-sense" account of state multiculturalism and disinvestment in services as analogous parts of the liberal state's betrayal of "authentic" East Enders'.[48] The rise of the BNP, as documented by Finn Gleeson, spoke to the racialised anxieties of an Isle of Dogs population whose day-to-day lives were forged by the 'tangible daily presence' of an empire which by the 1980s had ended, the remaining lifeworld subsequently torn apart by Thatcher's class war.[49]

In Liverpool, plagued by a similar set of structural problems to the Isle of Dogs, the enterprise zone also functioned as a crisis management strategy in the wake of the 1981 riots. Michael Heseltine authored *It Took A Riot!* in that same year, a revealing document, expressive of the period's mood music. Typical of the Thatcherite spatial regime, it advocated enterprise zones, unleashing the private sector, recommitting to law and order, promoting the service sector against Liverpool's ailing industrial economy and using the riots as an opportunity to wage a broader assault on any remaining municipal independence. It was intended as a tonic for the political illnesses bred by Liverpool council, run at the time by far-left militants.

Heseltine was clear that the Tories' housing policy would 'strike at the heart of Labour's concept of how society should be ordered'. As Secretary of State for Environment, he introduced policy favourable to the private sector, and to landlordism. He relaxed council housing regulations and rent controls, but crucially he introduced the New Right's flagship Right to Buy policy. Offering all local authority council tenants the right to purchase their home at discounted rates, averaging 44 per cent, Right to Buy was a hugely successful gambit. While sales were slow at first, by 1997 a third of Britain's 6 million council houses had been sold into private ownership. This rapid privatisation of the nation's housing stock, enabled by the 1980 Housing Act, was disproportionately taken up by middle-aged families – those in full-time manual or white collar work, people who knew other homeowners and had little interest in living in flats or next to council tenants. Buyers were ten times less likely to be unemployed than non-buyers.

Liberalising the mortgage market and driving down the building of council homes, Heseltine cleaved open a tension produced by 'property-owning social democracy'. Often considered, as Peter Malpass appropriately put it, the 'wobbly pillar of the welfare state', housing had come to exemplify the contradiction at the heart of state planning. Social democracy projected certain images of the good life, raising expectations about what the state could do and what kinds of consumerist existence were possible. But the half-hearted nature of reform, the volatility of the British economy, and the dogged resistance of employers who sought to deny workers' realisation of betterment through militant wage gains all combined to discredit the promises of Keynesianism. Instead, millions of people saw the realisation of the consumerist dream promised by postwar Labourism in the purchase of a home as a source of private affluence. In this sense, homeownership embodied a popular aspiration for security, mediated both by the failures of postwar social democracy and the social engineering of the New Right.

Thatcherism's enthusiasm for a property-owning democracy relied on representations of the population as divided between productive and independent citizens, on the one hand, and a parasitic and dependent underclass, on the other. This division cut right through the heart of the 'residualisation' of council housing, as Right to Buy took off in the South of England, in new towns and smaller rural districts, leaving behind the North West, London and other postindustrial urban centres. By the late 1980s, as Atkinson and Durden have documented, none of the fifteen local authorities which had sold more than 30 per cent of their housing stock were in the North East, Yorkshire and Humberside, the West Midlands, the North West or Inner London. This 'rollout' aspect of the New Right counter-revolution – which created a deeply unequal and uneven spatial economy as the basis for defeating the radical class subjects of the postwar moment – went hand in hand with a 'rollback' manoeuvre which crushed experiments in municipal socialism.

The introduction of the Local Government Act 1986 provided the Thatcherite regime with the tools necessary to destroy any remaining independence at the municipal level. The Conservatives shredded council funding; imposed caps on spending; centralised the collection of business rates, redistributing them according to Whitehall's diktats; enforced deregulation and outsourcing; and forced the selling-off of council housing stock, while central government kept the profits. The partially realised possibility of a unification between social movements, municipal socialist experiments like the GLC and the miners' strike didn't just constitute a threat to Thatcher; it also typified the potential of social alliances forged in mutual solidarity. The defeat of these battles portended a split in the imagination of working-class coalitional politics. Their routing signified the nail in the coffin of a conscious mutuality between regional class actors, left-wing municipalities and oppressed people, instead reinforcing the permanent incompatibility of these groups in the popular imagination.

Despite its success in destroying the fabric of Britain's diverse proletarian social worlds, the New Right also needed a positive agenda to sustain the disassembling of class agents it had augured. To this end, it sought ways to reproduce class actors as profitable, consenting cogs in the machine and not political agents. As early as 1982, the Conservatives were encouraging the population to use credit and debt, while abolishing credit controls and taking the first steps in the deregulation of financial markets. The financial liberalisation of the City of London and the launch of what the Iron Lady described as 'popular capitalism' – determined to 'enfranchise the many in the economic life of the nation' by enabling them to buy their council homes, take out private pension plans or purchase shares in privatised firms such as British Gas and British Telecom – was one means of embarking on what Jack Copley describes as 'depoliticised discipline', hemming the government into a ruthless tightening of the money supply precisely in order to curtail trade union strength and protect itself from popular opposition. Thatcher herself was explicit that the gambit would only work insofar as 'people believed in our determination to stick to it'.[50] And stick to it she did, deflating the economy and people's expectations that the course of the government could change. By liberalising financial markets, according to Leila Talani, this 'Big Bang represented the final stage of a process which had already begun in the mid-1970s: the definitive submission of productive capital to financial capital'.[51]

Crucially, this transition from a national productive economy to a nation state immersed in a world of global financialised flows opened pathways to modifying the means by which the population socially reproduced themselves. At the same time, it also gave austerian governments disciplinary rationales for hemming in demands for greater democratic power and better standards of living. Thatcher's exposition of a 'popular capitalism' was a strategy for undermining the prevailing Labourist vision of centralised state control of public resources; it also sought to reconstitute the subjectivity of British citizens around a competitive, entrepreneurial ethos. This Thatcherite social contract – which engineered the habits and interests of the population through low house prices, liberalised mortgage markets and low interest rates – did not so much overthrow Keynesian demand management as privatise it. Putting the burden of debt consumption on individuals rather than governments, increasing the availability of bank loans and credit cards, and raising the percentage of disposable household income made up by mortgages led sections of the working class to identify their life prospects with the fortunes of the City of London. In finance – as in industrial, welfare and urban policy – the duration and depth of neoliberal reforms aimed to transform the social, cultural and ideological fabric through which working-class subjects reproduced their lifeworlds. But to what extent had the Thatcherite regime been successful?

From the very outset, the New Right sought to mobilise ideology and material transformation together. As Stuart Hall wrote, the new Conservative politics depicted Labour as 'undividedly "with" the state and the power bloc' and Mrs Thatcher as 'undividedly, out there "with the people"'.[52] David Edgerton has demonstrated that the Conservatives inherited a nation self-sufficient in food, a net exporter of energy with millions of council homes to sell. Primed to take advantage of these conditions and the contingent windfalls it was bequeathed, the Conservative government raised over 2 billion pounds from the sales of council homes within its first four years, and considerably more from the sale of North Sea oil. In these circumstances, the Iron Lady and her supporters were able to wage a class war which would see the state withdraw almost entirely from industry. Thatcherite reforms had succeeded in facilitating a massive rebalancing of wealth between rich and poor, with the wealthy's income increasing by almost 60 per cent compared with a mere 6 to 13 per cent among the poor. There was a 10 per cent decline in the national debt and, utterly central to the regime's vision, the number of working days lost to strike action fell from 29 million in 1979 to just 761,000 in 1991, while union density in the workforce fell from 57 per cent to 42 per cent.

The labour market shaping Britain's political economy in the 1990s was markedly different from that inherited by Thatcher. The Fordist promise of a 'job for life' was replaced by Tory cabinet member Norman Tebbit's insistence that you 'get on your bike'. In March 1991, *The Employment Gazette* reported that only 5 million of Britain's workers were employed in manufacturing, with nearly 16 million in the service sector. Over a quarter of these service workers were employed in distribution, hotels, catering and repairs. The proliferation of longer working hours, reduced earnings, outsourcing, temporary contracts and employment agencies, all structured under the banner of 'flexible working', created a female-dominated labour market. This market absorbed sections of the redundant ex-manufacturing population, but also marketised conventional domestic tasks through the commodification of greater areas of social reproduction.

Among this new working class, despite the expansion of feminised service labour, the world of 'redundant masculinities' did not eliminate the substantial gap that existed in the carrying out of domestic duties. Women workers sold their labour more than they ever had in the previous forty-five years, but 67 per cent still carried out the tasks of social reproduction in the home according to the 1992 British Social Attitudes Survey. If they happened to be single mothers, as Helen Charman has revealed, they would face the freezing of one-parent benefits and the social pathologisation of their parental status by a Conservative moral panic over rising divorce rates. Additionally, the state of sick, older workers, reeling from the pressures of industrial life, worsened. While women workers became even more exposed to the stress, exhaustion and depression of the contemporary world of work, conditions such as asthma and vibration white finger – the ailments of the industrial worker – were superseded by musculoskeletal disorders and repetitive strain injuries as the common illnesses of a new, increasingly female, workforce.

With work failing to offer the promise of Keith Joseph's dream of 'embourgeoisement', the New Right's vision of 'popular capitalism' offered some limited solace. Between 1979 and 1991, the number of individual shareholders rose 18 per cent to 12.5 million people. Even though, according to Alexander Gallas, a 'substantial number only possessed small stakes and soon sold them' (and the proportion of shares in personal wealth rose a mere 1.7 per cent over the course of Thatcher's term), the work of interpellation had been achieved.[53] The 'two nations' project – of a productive, independent population ranged against its parasitic, dependent counterparts – had been effectively mobilised, pushing sections of an obsolete postindustrial class closer to the status of the black working class Enoch Powell had so famously demonised. The renovation of class power desired by the New Right, designed to rescue Britain from the claws of insurgent workers, radical feminists and militant black activists, had been achieved by stitching the imperatives of competition, propertarian impulses and hollow aspirationalism into the social fabric of a regionally, racially and politically stratified working class.

But the unattainability of the ideals of 'shareholder capitalism' for large parts of the proletariat, sandwiched between shit jobs, a surge in ill health and devastated lifeworlds, birthed newer, darker subjectivities. While some escaped and resisted Thatcherism and its heirs by embracing a popular, anti-authoritarian rave culture, this countercultural moment was by no means majoritarian. The tension at the heart of postwar social democracy – between the Keynesian demand management promise of proletarian consumer luxury and the developing reality of a state which could not deliver what the markets promised – was rearticulated by the New Right as a growing rift between property-owning workers in the booming South of England, and surplus populations with substantially less privatised relationships to housing in the rustbelt regions and inner cities. As Alexander Gallas has laid out, the high-tech and financial sector booms did not encompass huge parts of the West Midlands, South Wales, the North of England and Scotland, compounding mass unemployment in these regions and stymying the possibility of flight into work. In these classed situations, the New Right's counter-revolution threw many everyday phenomena into question, and new moral economies took hold.

For some sections of the population, like Oldham's Kashmiri and Pakistani textile workers, the mosque became the equivalent of the associational institutions – pubs, clubs, churches and co-ops – which sustained some ex-union white workers. Some Muslim workers were able to recommit themselves to Islam, unimpeded by factory time, finding meaning, support and escape in five-a-day prayer, fasting, family and community. If, as this chapter has argued, a necessary condition of neoliberalism in Britain was that it pulled the rug from beneath the feet of a radicalising collection of postwar subjects, then this phenomenon is characterised by the way the social environments of nation's postindustrial proletarians were, in the words of phenomenologist Simon J. Charlesworth, 'de-worlded'. According to the Rotherham native in a study of the psychological life of his hometown, the devastating realisation of Thatcher's 'affirmation trap' had produced a feeling of 'entrapment' through which the deteriorating living standards, crumbling infrastructure, state harassment and cheapening of life had come to exemplify a 'sense of inescapable destiny, of being individuals collectively overwhelmed by historical change'.[54] The defeat of the labour movement all but assured the decline of its associational culture, destroying so much of the social fabric that had guaranteed dignity and self-respect.

The erosion of these cultures spoke to a generalised sense of ruination. 'Living in a working-class area,' Charlesworth wrote, 'it is impossible not to confront the presence of a powerful force touching all of our lives.'[55] This overbearing, alienating force of capital tightening its grip over the sense of possibility, freedom and future among a whole community found its expression in the rise of crime, drug use, mental ill health and, far more commonly, resignation and powerlessness. The array of revived daily humiliations from the employer, the social security clerk and the police officer created new fears, anxieties and insecurities. The New Right had produced a new dehumanisation.

Articulated in Huw Beynon and Ray Hudson's *The Shadow of the Mine*, the paranoia of 'locking your doors' rapidly increased after the defeat of the miners' strike, signalling the emergence of new moral norms connected to people's exclusion from the formal economy.[56] The argument, made by Thatcher, that 'economics are the method; the object is to change the heart and soul', was foreshadowed by another phrase in the same *Sunday Times* interview. Just seconds before uttering her pithy mantra, this class warrior of historic proportions claimed that people had 'forgotten about the personal society' and were apparently left asking themselves, 'do I count, do I matter?'[57] The revolution in capitalist social relations engineered by her New Right – the ways in which they transformed militant subjects with a conception of freedom into powerless individuals with little claim to the future – has made that question ever more poignant, as individuals demand more of themselves in the absence of being able to ask more of the system. Thatcherism commenced a period of depleted living standards and shrunken political agency in which the common inability to earn more, buy a house and live even a narrowed version of the good life subjects us all to a lifetime of suspicion and moral recrimination. With capitalism's modes of impersonal domination and population management renovated, the 'personal society' had well and truly arrived.

4
The Long '90s Were Really Long

The class war is over.

Tony Blair, speech to Labour Party
Centenary Conference, 1999

By 1990, Thatcher had been thrown to the altar. The successful mass rebellion against her unpopular Poll Tax had discredited the Iron Lady, and the Black Wednesday financial crash destroyed the Conservatives' economic credentials, throwing millions of homes into negative equity and many more into poverty. The 'economic order politics' of Thatcherism were undermined by the sheer weight of its class politics. Despised across large parts of the country, internally fractured over the European question and its ability to manage the economy in doubt, the Conservative Party would face over a decade out of power. If Thatcher devastated the radical agents who desired the radicalisation and, in some cases, the transcendence of social democracy, then her successors across the benches of Parliament consolidated her regime and renewed it for a period of economic growth and thin optimism. The Iron Lady may have struck the fatal blows, but New Labour would erect the cage that trapped working-class politics in a zero-sum game.

Tony Blair and Gordon Brown's New Labour was a remarkable testament to how much the New Right had transformed the political landscape of the nation. By 1997, the country it was elected to govern had been transformed, and the party showed little interest in reversing the terms of Thatcher's mission. Despite the image it painted of itself as progressive, cool and chic, Blairism was fundamentally reactionary. One notable interlocutor of the gap between Blairite reality and representation was Stuart Hall. Briefly guilty of seeing some radical possibility in Blair's modernising ambitions, by 1997 Hall could see in Blair not just 'Thatcherism with a human face', but a 'conservative moderniser'. A 'personable young man', perhaps a 'post-feminist man', Hall's Blair presented an image of someone who may have grasped the 1960s and been friends with an unmarried mother, or even a victim of the AIDS epidemic. But once in power, despite increased social spending and progressive legal reforms on racial and sexual equality, it was clear that, 'on crime, on family values, on one-parent families, on questions of sexuality, on the particular variant of communitarianism' which he espoused, he gave '"modernity" such a deeply conservative inflection that it hardly' deserved the title.[1]

Rather than advancing a classically Labourist ambition to guide capitalism towards public good, New Labour repackaged Thatcherism in a language of progressive politics. Uneven economic development was aggregated on a regional basis in London's favour, and private finance initiatives were introduced into public education and the NHS. Taking advantage of the late-1990s credit boom, New Labour increased public spending even as it splintered Britain's social infrastructure. Spreading the gospel of market fundamentalism, the doyens of this new government insisted on wiring entrepreneurial ethos into the state, spinning commodification as the devolution of power. Selling off assets like the London Underground and national transport, Blair's march through the institutions prioritised competition, dressing up private profiteering in the language of 'efficiency' and 'choice'. Its approach to local councils would, as Tom Crewe argues, 'leave almost all the new restrictions in place, to encourage more outsourcing and to place ever tighter controls on funding'. The social devastation left in the wake of industry's demise under Thatcher was only exacerbated under New Labour, which reproduced democratic disenfranchisement through the growth of a particular variant of right-wing neoliberal Labourism in local municipal institutions, and developed new shields for central government. As Hall noted in his damnatory article 'New Labour's Double-Shuffle', Blairism had rearticulated the language of reform to mean counter-reform, projecting regressive shifts in favour of private business as radical paths towards a progressive futurity. In all but name, Labour's transformation throughout the 1990s is best understood as an attempt to consolidate the New Right's project through a kind of managed neoliberalism.

When it came to Blair's work regime, the legal minimum wage and mildly improved rights over unfair dismissal and union recognition were introduced without undermining any of the New Right's vast apparatus of anti-union laws. In the twenty years since Thatcher had been elected, low-skilled occupations had undergone extensive growth. Numbers of retail cash desk and checkout operators had almost doubled; care assistants and attendants looking after the sick, old and disabled had risen by well over 400,000; and waiters, waitresses, bar staff, shelf fillers and sales assistants had all significantly risen as proportions of the labour market. Total state and para-state jobs (such as social provision in the private sector) had risen by millions, with the majority of these in health and social care, but the number of manufacturing workers had dropped further and faster than in any other European industrial country. Once the 'workshop of the world', Britain could now be neatly described, heeding the analysis of David Harvey, as a system of 'flexible accumulation'.[2]

Workers were subject to the extraction of what Marx termed 'absolute surplus value'. Two decades of neoliberal policy had extended the working day relative to wages, reduced the standard of living and moved production overseas in search of propitious conditions. John Maynard Keynes's 1930 projection that the grandchildren of his contemporaries would only work fifteen-hour weeks was miserably upended as the millennium approached. Under the weight of labour market deregulation and with the erosion of collective bargaining, workers toiled a mere hour and a half less than their forebears had in 1970. The introduction of new technologies cut labour costs, expanded workplace surveillance and created bifurcations between workers who could operate new technologies and those who could not. This 'flexible accumulation' strategy created a stressed labour force, working in harsh, competitive conditions.

This was exacerbated by Blairism's commitment to diminishing the power of those groups of powerful workers which had outlasted Thatcher. Aware of the enduring militancy and close social ties between workers at Royal Mail, for example, New Labour and Royal Mail bosses, most notably in this period former Saatchi & Saatchi CEO Adam Crozier, were intent on 'laying the groundwork' for privatisation, liberalising the postal services market, and breaking Royal Mail's monopoly. This manifested in a number of ways on the shopfloor. According to former Royal Mail worker Joe McCluskey, 'there was cuts every year', with this state-owned company being run on 'cut-throat principles, squeezing as much out of you as they possibly can'. Panicked about the need to eliminate 'Spanish practices' – a term denoting the range of workforce cultures seemingly holding back productivity and profitability – Crozier and the Labour government sought to set the pace for privatisation by growing voluntary redundancies, transforming the delivery service, and pursuing control over workers' time and labour processes. With the rollout of voluntary redundancies as one key mechanism for cutbacks, the Communication Workers Union would claim that negotiating down the number of older workers accepting relatively large redundancy payments was a victory. But, as Joe narrates to me, this would become increasingly tenuous as a method for halting privatisation and encroaching employer power, as with each redundancy more responsibility and work would fall on the laps of fewer workers, creating – alongside the recruitment of younger workers from outside the tight-knit lifeworlds of the postal service – weaker forms of bargaining power on behalf of the workforce. For Joe, connecting wage rises to voluntary redundancies placed a straitjacket around the union, making it less capable of struggling against Labour rollbacks, Tory-era privatisation and restructuring accelerated by the rise of Parcelforce and, later, Amazon.

These changes and struggles within Royal Mail also mirrored wider transformations in the contemporary workplace. Large supermarket chains such as Tesco represented the vast expansion, concentration and rationalisation of the retail industry, employing over 159,000 workers in the year New Labour was elected. As the promise of transferring obsolescent cohorts of former industrial workers into new manufacturing hubs waned, vast legions of workers were absorbed into services and elementary occupations, signalling the rising commodification of social reproduction in the wake of privatisation and the whittling of the Keynesian social wage. As Kevin Doogan has observed, the rise of new forms of surveillance and electronic point-of-sale technologies went hand in hand with the recomposition of work. Swelling economies of scale produced new patterns of part-time and temporary employment, structured around the surge in twenty-four-hour shopping and the creeping intrusion of private firms: Virgin took over the railways, Tesco bought petrol stations and WH Smith rented space in train stations. While full-time work still predominated, higher rates of exploitation among women and the young in the wake of over a decade of high levels of unemployment and scaled-down legal protections made life worse for workers at the turn of the century.

The 1999 *Job Insecurity and Work Intensification* report, commissioned by the Joseph Rowntree Foundation, offered a grim image of working-class perception. Sixty per cent of respondents expressed frustrations with speed-ups on the shopfloor, 40 per cent displayed little trust for their employers and the report conveyed a general anxiety over the hostile conditions which confronted people in the event of job loss. In particular, the survey identified 'stress' as a consequence of increased efficiency, mirroring both the intensification of exploitation and the strikingly miserable life chances which confronted those unlucky enough not to be exploited. In 1998, the Bristol Stress and Health at Work Study noted that one in five workers 'believed their jobs were extremely or very stressful, such that this level of stress was making them ill'. From the high labour turnover in Britain's multiplying call centres to heightening reports of 'stress' across the labour market, proletarians confronted depression, anxiety attacks, musculoskeletal disorders and 'heightened risk of coronary heart disease, stomach ulcers and some cancers'.[3] The kinds of sickness and disablement impacting workers reflected a transformed labour market, a mushrooming of new kinds of work, and a shift in the balance of power between labour and capital – that is, they were the structure of feeling that defined the proletarian experience of New Labour's managed neoliberalism.

Workers' worries were reinforced by the insecurity baked into New Labour's acceleration of Thatcherite welfare reforms. When New Labour took office in 1997, they inherited an official unemployment rate of just under 2 million. According to a comprehensive study by Christina Beatty et al., real unemployment was almost 4 million.

Facing that challenge, Tony Blair argued that reducing the dole queue would 'be easier' if the labour market were 'working properly'. What was needed, in the view of New Labour ideologues, was the reinforcement of a 'low-wage sector' predicated on low-skilled jobs readily accessible to those on welfare.

Although New Labour stalled the spiralling immiseration commenced by Thatcher's war on workers, its minimum-wage regulations, increased child benefits and introduction of tax credits did not reverse the trend. Inheriting predecessor John Major's means-tested and conditional Jobseeker's Allowance, Blairism's commitment to workfare and obligatory training programmes was central to a policy programme that sought to provide a steady supply of precarious, low-paid workers to the service sector. According to Bernhard Rieger, New Labour's rejigging of the welfare system involved a move towards a welfare state best characterised as a 'new Speenhamland' system. The original Speenhamland system, the backdrop to Karl Polanyi's *The Great Transformation*, saw the payment of wages below survival levels subsidised through the Poor Laws rate system. If that sounds like a very non-neoliberal moral economy, it was in fact recreated under neoliberalism in an effort to subsidise employers, weaken worker power and stymie the problem of poverty.

Accompanying this new welfare system, a ramped-up moral panic targeted 'benefit scroungers', while Blair railed against a 'sick note culture'. As Secretary of State for Work and Pensions, Alistair Darling condemned a 'something for nothing culture'. New Labour increased spending on welfare for deeply classed, non-redistributive purposes with one hand, and held up a megaphone decrying benefit claimants with the other. Blair's party introduced Anti-Social Behaviour Orders to monitor unemployed urban youth and attacked single mothers, stressing the need for them to restrain themselves from having more children. Helen Charman's *Mother*

State captures the reactionary mood at the time, wherein single mothers 'were accused of ... producing a child to extract support from the surrogate paternal state'.[4] In this reading, a campaign of demonisation took Britain's relatively high teenage pregnancy rate and mobilised it against a section of the population deemed a sponge on welfare and a hurdle to cultivating a slick labour market. Blair's emphasis on 'strong families' as units of production, the New Deal for Lone Parents and sex education in schools all cultivated a reactionary environment geared towards the proliferation of amenable forms of particularly feminised wage labour.

In the minds of New Labour intellectuals like Andrew Adonis, the logic that a rising tide lifts all boats meant that 'the old labels of "working-" and "middle-class" make less and less sense'.[5] But in reality, the conscious ideological erosion of these categories by Blairism's spin doctors recreated notions of who was included in the national community. The suggestion that the working class no longer existed signalled that those who could not achieve private affluence were feckless, undeserving or, as Owen Jones has documented, 'chavs'. In *Redundant Masculinities?*, Linda McDowell details how younger, often male workers found themselves at a relative disadvantage compared with more experienced workers, given the exposure of their jobs and of youth training schemes to economic restructuring. The heightened vulnerability of young employees to low wages increased their dependency on parents and the state, thereby stretching the economic experience of youth far beyond the period of life it characterised for previous postwar generations.

These phenomena were rationalised by the intellectual core of New Labour, figures such as Anthony Giddens and Frank Field, in an attempt to theorise and respond to what the Child Poverty Action Group described as 'social exclusion'. Importing US debates over a 'culture of poverty' into Britain, best encapsulated by the racialising psychodramas of the Democrat-drafted *Moynihan Report*, which demonised black mothers as 'welfare queens', proponents of New Labour insisted that culture had just as much of a role to play in the decline of communities as economics did. According to Giddens, the dilapidation of housing, persistent unemployment and the rise in 'antisocial behaviour' were evidence that postindustrial populations needed to be engineered away from 'cycles of poverty' and towards training, education and, most importantly, employment opportunities. Thus Field, a Christian socialist-inspired Labour MP, reconsidered the emphasis New Labour's progressive neoliberalism placed on self-help, arguing that welfare had to be focused on reconstituting the behaviour of society's most deprived in a way that maximised their output. He insisted that 'welfare influences behaviour by the simple device of bestowing rewards (benefits) and allotting punishments (loss of benefits) ... the nature of our character depends in part on the values which welfare fosters'.[6] From this vantage point, disintegrating community fabrics opened the way for a punitive welfare system geared towards deterring crime and incentivising obedience to the demands of the labour market.

These new policy tools, defined by a research agenda which included measurements such as 'low birth-weight babies, problem drug use (ages 15 to 24), suicide (ages 15 to 24), obesity, limiting longstanding illness or disability, and non-participation in civic organisations', drove a new regime of population management.[7] New Labour's painting of this social cohort, particularly its younger layers, as an ASBO generation of 'yobs' unable to compete in Britain's increasingly affluent and levelled political economy, combined with the spread of multiculturalism and interracial friendship groups among the young, provided the ingredients for Powellite representations of a labour market entry process which belied the reality of disempowered workers, intensified competition and the absence of futurity experienced by young people.

But for a portion of workers, relatively fortunate in their labour market location, the economic boom which fuelled Labour's new-millennium optimism was predicated on forms of privatised welfare. In the absence of the kinds of profitable ventures which had characterised manufacturing in the twentieth century, investment took a rapid lurch towards financialised assets, chasing short-term returns over long-term investments in fixed, productive capital. Financialisation presented the possibility that the postwar social-democratic project of high wages, a welfare state and Keynesian demand management could be short-circuited by extending market risks to 'ordinary consumers via extended mortgages and credit card debt'.[8] Essential for buttressing the inequalities of the labour market, New Labour made asset-based welfare policies a staple of its social contract. In its 2001 election manifesto, Tony Blair's party committed to making assets a 'fourth pillar' of the welfare state. The primary location for Blairism's asset-based welfarism was the home, with assets replacing the wobbly fourth pillar of social housing.

House-price dynamics, or 'house-price Keynesianism', functioned as a form of subjectivation that reorganised the habits of large sections of the population to emphasise 'property-owning democracy' as the staple of the social contract. Imagined as a civic right, inflating house prices promised to facilitate the citizens' present and secure their future. British homeowners took to 'banking' on their properties, releasing equity and remortgaging to supplement pensions, meet essential repairs and secure their own needs. Aided by 'new mortgage products that facilitated drawdown from accumulated housing wealth', the integration of housing, mortgage and financial markets created a situation in which state pensions and earnings from work dwindled as forms of social security. In their place, housing wealth and private pensions constituted 78 per cent of personal sector wealth by 2006–8. More than an economic shift or bubble, this extension and financialisation of Thatcher's property-owning democracy aimed to produce a new subjectivity among large layers of the population. A social worldview in which your pension, your care home and your child's prospects could all be subject to your capacity to borrow against an asset (namely your house) marked a distinct shift in both the form and space of capitalist population management.

Shored up by low interest rates, cheap credit and a slackening of housebuilding, the Treasury under Blair actively oriented itself towards the creation of conditions which would increase 'self-reliance in the long-term', 'enhance people's capacity to be more independent' and 'encourage people to build an asset up so that they can think about their future in a different way'.[9] Putting the burden of state planning onto the individual, New Labour was, as Matthew Watson has detailed, creating subjects invested in 'saving for a rainy day', where the promise of future economic security was no longer assured by collective welfare provision, but by one's ability to act as an investor. The formation of this 'investor subjectivity' provided the state with the capacity to mould 'the private space of the home' into the 'public space' not of the national economy but, as Watson argues, into one small cog in a financialised global economy.[10]

This rendition of managed neoliberalism, with aggregated individual debt acting as a driver of economic growth, was mirrored in New Labour's broader spatial regime. Between 1995 and 2005, Britain was consumed by a global housing boom which saw house prices rise by 133 per cent. Blairism, particularly in New Labour's second term, was focused on ensuring the continuation of this boom, which it sought to do by expanding private housing construction, facilitating popular owner-occupation and scaling down social housing. In the 2004 report *UK Mortgage Market: Taking the Long-Term View*, the Treasury was marked out as being involved in encouraging shared equity, further deregulating the housing market and setting a homeownership target of 75 per cent of housing tenure. Over the course of Tony Blair's term as prime minister, average house prices tripled, borrowing costs increased as a result and private renting grew as a share of housing. As a direct result, younger workers increasingly struggled to get into the housing market as the 2000s progressed. Despite 'house-price Keynesianism' enticing first-time buyers to get onto the housing ladder (80 per cent relied on some injection of family money), the number of young first-time buyers declined by 40 per cent between 1986 and 2005, and owner-occupation in general also began to fall as a proportion of tenure.

This uneven process of declassing, shedding public welfare provision through the privatisation of everyday life, was also accompanied by what Owen Hatherley has described as 'class cleansing'.[11] Across England, from Stoke-on-Trent to Tyneside and back across the rustbelt, working-class areas left to rot by the collapse of steel, coal and other forms of manufacturing and underwhelmed by the failed promise of industry's return, in advanced, high-tech form, experienced social decline on an unprecedented scale. Instead of class solidarity, labour movement resurgence, the cutting edge of industry and a social wage, workers faced poverty pay in warehouses, dilapidated housing and chronic underinvestment. According to Mike Makin-Waite, in 1990s Burnley, where the gross annual income of almost half of households was less than £15,000, the confluence of depopulation, negative equity and speculators buying up property that they then did nothing with, produced unprofitable housing markets. In the context of this spatially uneven decline, 'regeneration' was embraced as the new buzzword of Labour governments, posed as the solution to the classed moral panics that targeted communities seemingly distinguished by the marks of alcoholism, drug addiction and criminality.

Between 2002 and 2011, party grandee John Prescott initiated the Housing Market Renewal Pathfinders scheme, which took power away from local authorities and enacted a national slum clearance project, spanning towns and cities from Birmingham up to Sheffield, Newcastle and Liverpool, by enforcing compulsory repurchasing and demolishing hundreds of thousands of homes. Carried out under the auspices of reviving abandoned communities, this initiative was geared towards rectifying 'market failure'. It sought to hoist up the property market as a model of economic growth and aspiration, reproducing the English South's affluence in the country's rustbelt. According to Andrew McCulloch, by stitching neoliberal urban policy onto Area Based Initiatives, the national government could claim that it was involving local communities, when instead it created public–private partnerships, collaborating with property developers and partner agencies who had 'an ideological and material interest in representing the fact that there is a community for which they act'.[12] Engineered by the logics of New Labour's Social Exclusion Unit, decades-old communities were torn apart and rehoused in different locations under the banner of, in Prescott's words, 'building sustainable communities'.

In Liverpool, as in other places, the Pathfinder scheme signalled disaster. As planner and member of Merseyside Civic Society Jonathan Brown documents, vast sums of public money were wasted as housing association heads received lofty bonuses and six-figure salaries to 'decant their stock' of tenants. Elderly owner-occupiers were stripped of equity, whole streets were left derelict, with thousands displaced, and waiting lists for housing ballooned. A demonstrable failure, top-down public–private planning had made the fundamental mistake of thinking that a housing boom could be replicated in parts of the country that witnessed no concomitant boom in jobs and opportunities. Capturing the approach of those engineering this calamity, Brown recollects one Pathfinder boss describing Liverpool as an 'urban hell' in front of a Manchester conference. Instead of refurbishment and local improvement, social landlords, property developers and state officials opted for a policy of resolving Thatcherite organised abandonment by displacing the residents of one site and spreading the reach of abandonment to many more areas at a far more molecular level.

In this sense, the Pathfinder scheme did not just imitate New Labour's inclination towards asset-based welfare – it also evidenced its disdain towards those sections of the working class who could not take advantage of the promise of a marketised social safety net. Unlike Thatcher's model before it, Labour's managed neoliberalism may not have been fundamentally concerned with the threat posed by these communities, but the party was keen to reshape the social fabric of capitalism, opening up new opportunities for growth and accumulation, and making it clear that these missions were bearing fruit. New Labour sought to make spatial Thatcherism work where it otherwise had not. Even where it failed, as it did catastrophically in the case of the Pathfinder scheme, New Labour was keen to project an image of itself as a sleek, glowing entrepreneurial success against the hauntologies of a criminal underclass unable to rise to the occasion. Blairism's attempt to bridge the gap between Thatcher's successful class war and her failed reformation of British capitalism played out on one terrain in particular: real estate.

One arena in which the picture of Blairism as cosmopolitan to its core would crumble was, ironically enough, in its own self-presentation as an advocate of multiculturalism. Despite the 'Cool Britannia' aesthetic of Blairism, which sought to paint a vision of postcolonial nationhood absent the attachment to whiteness, the country's 'multicultural drift' proved too troublesome for New Labour. What Stuart Hall identified as 'globalisation from below' – typified in the spectacle of 'white wannabees' speaking in patois, listening to Hip-Hop or later Grime – provoked a growing elite fear that the fabric of the once respectable working class had been tainted by the diversity otherwise officially celebrated in New Labour ideology.[13]

A growing concern for Tony Blair and his coterie was that a section of the electorate, insecure in their fortunes and anxious about migrants and asylum seekers as destabilising threats, were in need of appeasement. A gradual influx of Roma migrants into the country via Dover beginning in 1997 tested New Labour's progressive rhetoric. Making huge sacrifices to come to Britain, these migrants were met with scorn by politicians and pundits. A flurry of newspaper stories about 'bogus asylum seekers' became headlines decrying the 'INVASION OF THE GIRO CZECHS'. The local Labour MP Gwyn Prosser claimed that 'the behaviour of some claiming asylum has been abominable', repeating the mantra that they were 'actually bogus asylum seekers'. In the face of this moral panic, as Richard Power Sayeed writes in *1997*, the 'Home Office buckled, announcing that individuals appealing against rejection of their asylum applications would now have only five days – cut drastically from twenty-eight – before immigration officials "bounced" them out of the country'.[14] The swiftness of Home Secretary Jack Straw's response was roundly celebrated by the political right.

Under the rubric of the home secretary's claim that the electorate 'wanted to know that our borders were controlled, that the system was in safe hands', a new racial regime was constructed. To this end, the Immigration and Asylum Act 1999 granted the home secretary new powers. As Nadine El-Enany highlights, under this legislation, 'a new social category of asylum seeker' was born and in the process separated from 'recognised refugees' both in 'policy and popular discourse'.[15] As well as imposing a voucher scheme on all claimants, the legislation implemented a new system of forced dispersal intended to limit the visibility of racialised people through a process of removal and distribution. Asylum seekers were coerced into the poorest parts of the country under threat of removal. This strategy, identified by journalist Daniel Trilling as the dispersal of the 'migration problem' to the towns and cities in which the zero-sum impulses of neoliberal defeat and competition were most keenly felt, mirrored a broader sense of breakdown that had emerged in the millennium-era politicisation of state multiculturalism.

In 2001, the year New Labour was elected to its second term in government, race riots involving thousands broke out across Oldham, Bradford and later Burnley. Sparked by the agitations of far-right groups such as the BNP, the National Front and Combat 18, clashes erupted across the Pennines, between Asian youth, their white counterparts and riot police. In these postindustrial towns, where wage labour was once *the* rare aspect of life connecting white and Asian workers, the state multiculturalism of the neoliberal era presided over forms of social segregation rather than the urban hybridisation of the bigger cities. In the mills, white workers might have worked the day shift, while their Pakistani and Kashmiri counterparts worked nights, but the job constituted a fragile sinew holding a segregated town together. Colin Webster highlights how the disappearance of the factories exacerbated the 'geographical concentrations of fear, risk and insecurity' which underpinned racist violence and ethnic conflict. Oldham's racialised segregation was realised in the windswept valley tops, referred to as the 'white highlands', and the valley bottoms that housed South Asian communities.[16] The subsequent Cantle Report captured the image, with a Muslim of Pakistani origin stating they would 'not see another white face until I come back here next week', and a young man from a white council estate declaring he had 'never met anyone on this estate who wasn't like us from around here'.[17] The correlation of 'white flight' and South Asian concentration fuelled images of abandonment, as Asians rightly viewed the rise of racial incidents from 13,151 in 1996–7 to 52,694 in 2003–4 through the lens of racist hostility, while whites explained social decline through the language of inter-ethnic competition.

The reality was that state multiculturalism created a class of community leaders who presided over a system of scarce resources. This institutional structure presented an opportunity for forces such as the BNP to project an image of some communities being prioritised over others. In the process, a renewed nationalist movement injected a politics of negative solidarity into a disintegrating social world absolutely ripe for it. As Mike Makin-Waite has narrated in *On Burnley Road*, the far right mobilised the iconography of Old Labourism, 'the Labour Party that your grandfathers voted for', in order to construct a 'demoralised class politics' built around a nostalgic, exclusionary whiteness.[18] The Cantle Report, written in the wake of the milltown riots, identified a segregated but competitive and mutually recriminatory existence between racialised minorities and white majorities in postindustrial towns. Its solution was a focus on state-orchestrated 'community cohesion', emphasising 'social order', 'community values' and 'regeneration' and reinforcing the contours of British citizenship.[19]

Appropriately enough, given New Labour's attempt to rearticulate citizenship away from a dependence on public services, Ted Cantle was the lead in new Home Secretary David Blunkett's Community Cohesion Review Team. The priority of this team became the assimilation of migrant communities, corroborating, according to Bridget Anderson, the state's broader emphasis on 'naturalising' new arrivals whose cultures were represented as out of kilter with the broader national community. This 'reflexive multiculturalism' insisted on imposing integration on minority communities. But in something of a catch-22, at the same time as it pathologised South Asian communities in the north of England for their failure to dissolve their cultures into Britishness, the Labour government bemoaned the lived multiculture of the big cities for its effect on the white citizenry. Jack Straw's claim, in the wake of the invasions of Afghanistan and Iraq and the accompanying Islamophobic War on

Terror, that the Muslim woman's choice to wear a Hijab signalled 'a visible statement of separation and difference' was a practical outcome of the Cantle Report's drive towards 'community cohesion'. This, in a context in which cohesion only ever looked like a nebulous and segregated image of 'British culture'.[20]

This environment witnessed the displacement of anti-racism as a force capable of critiquing the power structures. The organisers of state multiculturalism asserted that the challenges facing postindustrial towns had little to do with economics or power, but were instead products of the cultures of the communities who inhabited them, both brown and white. Indicatively, the portrayal of Muslims as a disruptive, counter-civilisational force in need of monitoring and surveillance through the state's authoritarian PREVENT agenda, mimicked New Labour's dour representation of deprived working-class communities pathologically unable to find permanent work or get on the housing ladder. The perceived inability of both groups to cohere amid a briefly growing British capitalism that was embarking on imperial adventures abroad placed them outside the legitimate space of the national fabric. In the worldview of New Labour's managed multiculturalism, segregated South Asian terraces sat next to the white working-class redbrick and the multiracial inner-city estate as imagined ghettos, or nations within the nation, all sources of demographic anxiety that exemplified broader concerns, also prevalent on the right, about the nation's *longue duree* decline. As Lentin and Titley have noted, these 'micro-spatial' panics are metaphors for a macroeconomic story about Britain's inability to reassert its dwindling postimperial influence on the world stage, in which it had become one weakened outpost of civilisation among many, marginalised from without and diluted from within. This was a familiar story of postimperial decline working by means of racialisation.

Under New Labour, the rollout of ASBOs, the ramping up of stop-and-search powers and a raft of repressive counter-terrorism measures all heralded a period which saw 3,600 new criminal offences created and a 66 per cent rise in the prison population between 1997 and 2010. Within this rubric, multiculturalism became less about the diverse co-existence of different ethnicities, and more about the incorporation of difference into a homogeneous national bloc of repressed unity. The treatment of racialised minorities, the melding of their status and place in the nation, collided with the evolving offer of national citizenship in general. For example, Tony Blair's fearmongering in 2004 that the nation was reaching a 'tipping point' dovetailed with Eastern European accession into the EU and the subsequent rise in migration from the continent into Britain.[21] Between 1995 and 2014, the share of immigrants among working-age adults in the UK more than doubled, from 8 per cent to 17 per cent, over 6.5 million in total.

Framed, as Anderson describes, through the lens of a '"degenerate" whiteness', Eastern Europeans, like Jews and the Irish before them, were quickly coded as competitors, scroungers and insufficiently European. When looked at in this respect, the multiple vectors of racialisation organised and articulated by New Labour aggravated the disentangling of anti-racism from working-class politics begun under Thatcherism. 'British values' became a proxy for reconstituting racialised outsiders and foreign interests against the supposedly conservative cultures and values of the deserving white worker. Blairism was disastrous for workers and the poor, and it fed the caricatures of class, race and identity which would become so central to British politics throughout the next decade. If you were working class, a racialised minority, a single mother, a welfare claimant or disabled, Blair's Labour simply made you feel like you weren't worth it, and that you were always responsible for the problems of your compatriots and the country-at-large. The class-fracturing effects of spatial Thatcherism – already exacerbated by New Labour's aggressive embrace of City-led growth, and scarcely mitigated by its 'regional development' schemes – were further worsened by the racial management politics arising from the party's response to the northern riots and its policing of Muslim minorities. If these reconstituted cultural antagonisms lacked a language of class, Gordon Brown's term as prime minister and his subsequent handling of the great financial crash would fill that absence in even more nativist terms.

In 2007, the buoyant optimism which had characterised a booming global economy came to a cataclysmic end. The preponderance of 'fictitious capital', in the form of derivatives (bets hedged on the direction of future assets, securitised into collateralised debt obligations), required the growth of mortgage and debt markets. This securitised debt, equalling $1 trillion at the turn of the century, rose to $2.7 trillion within five years. By 2007, as US workers defaulted on their mortgage schemes, global capitalism descended into its worst crisis in a lifetime. The virus of credit default took down bank after bank, from Lehman Brothers to Northern Rock; sent major firms such as General Motors into bankruptcy; and threw millions of people across the planet out of work and onto dole queues. In Britain alone, the number of unemployed workers would rise to 2.7 million, while almost 50,000 homes would be repossessed. A succession of governments across the Global North, including Brown's Labour administration, responded to the crash by rescuing the banks and socialising the losses, turning private debt public so as to rescue capitalism from itself. This rescue package resulted in a £157 billion government deficit. In the words of David McNally, as the global supply of money and credit contracted, this bailout did not end the economic crisis of 2008–9 – instead, the crisis simply 'mutated'.[22]

In the wake of the crash, the bailing out of the banks and the first major sign of the disintegration of the global economic order, Gordon Brown tried to rearticulate British nationalism in one last gasp of an exhausted New Labour. The first words uttered by Brown on his ascendancy to the British premiership in 2007, 'British jobs for British workers', became an attempt to recalibrate New Labour's image in the wake of the financial crash. Constructing an image of 'us' and 'them' on the labour market, the former Chancellor of the Exchequer was articulating, as Anderson has demonstrated, what he thought a good British job consisted of, and what work he considered Britain's underclasses and racialised minorities deserving of. When this nativist lurch was met with support among striking workers across manufacturing and construction sites, particularly at the Lindsey Oil Refinery in Lincoln, a huge argument erupted among some of the most organised sectors of the trade union movement. Unite leader Derek Simpson was even photographed with the right-wing *Daily Star* next to the nationalist 'British jobs for British workers' banner. While a common cause was eventually made between migrant workers and English workers, isolating the influence of trade union racism and the divisive efforts of the fascist BNP, Brown's speech would set a precedent for political actors seeking to reanimate a nationalist class politics in the wake of neoliberalism's disintegration. The BNP's adoption of the slogan at the next general election was just a taste of how race and class would be articulated together in a reactionary fashion throughout the next decade.

The implosion of New Labour's millennium-era confidence exposed a dark imperative that was always central to the project's ambitions: for those not easily embedded in a population of pliable, insecure workers wedded to British values, hard work and the family unit, demonisation awaited. To come of age under this settlement was to find oneself in a cultural prison. My mother was forced off benefits under John Major's assault on single mothers, the uprooting of working-class communities through the Pathfinder scheme was mirrored in the transformation and breaking apart of seemingly problematic communities across the London I grew up in, and my black and Muslim friends were subject to a routine campaign of police harassment and vilification that would have made Enoch Powell proud.

In many ways, those of us who did not fit neatly into Blairism's remit of acceptable subjects ran the risk of descending into abjection. Culturally, Labour's time in power was adorned by the demeaning, ableist, class spite of *Little Britain* and *The Catherine Tate Show*, the ritual humiliations of *The Jeremy Kyle Show* and the marginalisation of the DIY cultures of the urban poor, notably Grime. Dizzee Rascal's claim on his seminal debut album, *Boy in da Corner*, 'I'm a problem for Anthony Blair', struck right at the heart of New Labour's relationship to those it deemed unworthy. It was an incredibly difficult time to be working class, let alone to belong to those quarters of the proletariat who did not work in relatively secure conditions, enter the property market or escape the perils of organised abandonment.

Appropriately, New Labour was succeeded by an austerian Conservative-led cabinet, which only had to repurpose the cultural tools weaponised by New Labour against society's poor. For all Blair's talk of progress, community cohesion and civilising the world, New Labour was a deeply radicalising project which exacerbated the racialised recrimination that has dominated British politics throughout the twenty-first century. At the same time, it also produced a backlash, dominant in the decades to come, of a generation of people, like myself, unwilling to accept the zero-sum, cultural revanchism Blair and Brown spent so much political capital trying to triangulate and reproduce. This regime would exacerbate the democratic decline and political decomposition of the nation's classes, marshalling forms of *disorganised* abandonment in the process, which would be, as already demonstrated in Chapter Two, felt, read and responded to differently depending on one's place and position in society. After New Labour, nothing would be the same again, and none of the old guarantees of class politics would remain.

5
Whither Gravediggers?

What the bourgeoisie therefore produces, above all, are its own grave-diggers. Its fall and the victory of the proletariat are equally inevitable.

The Manifesto of the Communist Party,
Karl Marx and Friedrich Engels

In 1868, in a letter penned to German social democrat Ludwig Kugelmann, Karl Marx opined on his theory of class: 'I represent large-scale industry not only as the mother of antagonism, but also as the creator of the material and spiritual conditions necessary for the solution of this antagonism.'[1] According to Marx, in order to create a productive population capable of accumulating wealth, the bourgeois class had cultivated a set of power arrangements contingent on the coordination and centralisation of labour, with him and Engels remarking in 'The Communist Manifesto', that this 'revolutionary combination' would stifle the competitive isolation of proletarian life. This was Marx's theory of the revolutionary class. The three conditions underpinning this theoretical wager on the proletariat as the revolutionary class capable of transcending capitalism were its centrality to the production of wealth, its own lack of wealth and ownership, and the socialised industrial experience and collective consciousness augured by industrialisation. What the nineteenth-century bourgeoisie had produced, above all, were their own gravediggers.

So far, this book has narrated a succession of breakdowns and transformations in capitalist population management. The neoliberal social contract which based the population's access to housing, care and consumption goods on its capacity to acquire cheap credit is now in deep trouble. The ills raging throughout Britain and across large parts of the planet, from high interest rates and expensive housing costs to demographic ageing, runaway climate change and economic stagflation, are a product of this social contract and will be its demise. The erection of this neoliberal settlement, just like its disintegration, has produced a range of subjects distinct from those who lived and breathed throughout Marx's lifetime. In that spirit, we should ask ourselves again the questions which conditioned Marx's theory of the revolutionary class. Do most workers in this country produce society's wealth in the sense that Marx documented in *Capital*, and what are the implications of this? Do working-class people today have nothing to lose but their chains? And how has the lived reality of both social democracy and neoliberalism charted in this book changed the collective experience Marx and Engels observed in Britain's large-scale nineteenth-century industrial battalions?

From Marx's time onwards, the coalescence of large pools of workers into bigger combines has often been aligned with forms of competition between workers on economic lines, often refracted through racialised and gendered rationalisations such as the undercutting of wages, the replacement of one group of workers with another, or forms of workplace segregation. When Karl Marx lived in Britain, the largest share of the workforce – feminised domestic labourers – were fundamentally unproductive of wealth-creating value. Today, within a labour market stratified by race, gender, nation and much else, commodified social reproduction has been drawn into the remit of productive value chains. Capital's domination over the labour process, the lack of investment in manufacturing and the massively expanded demand for cheap consumer goods, all defining features of the post-1979 settlement, have produced large pools of circulatory labour, such as service proletarians and logistics workers, alongside even larger layers of socially reproductive labour. It is important to disentangle these categories, and complicate them: 'services' is a nebulous euphemism which collapses a great deal of varied human labour into one, homogeneous bloc; logistics workers, an indispensable component of global supply chains, are among the most powerful workers in the world; and workers in the realm of social reproduction *could* include anyone from the nurse to the nanny.

While contemporary capitalism, particularly in tertiary service economies such as Britain, is in no way capable of the kinds of economic growth and formal productive heights achieved from the late nineteenth century to the immediate postwar years, this concomitant process of deindustrialisation and stagnation, paralleled with the entrance of women workers into the labour market in growing numbers, has commodified greater swathes of everyday life. In sum, larger numbers are, according to Anwar Shaikh and Ertuğrul Ahmet Tonak, 'capitalistically organised', pulled into the increasingly massifying spaces of value-producing labour chains oriented towards our reproduction as human beings.[2]

One claim, made by Marxist labour scholar Kim Moody, is that the neoliberal period has witnessed the types of capital concentration apparent in Marx's oeuvre, with industrial cores, shooting off into 'concentric circles', assembling an array of nodes, clusters, metropolitan areas and working-class neighbourhoods, which resemble the great value-producing agglomerations of Detroit's twentieth-century assembly plants or, closer to home, the car plants of postwar

Coventry. The process, as far as Moody is concerned, which sees value move from the production and refining of raw materials to the checkout counter at Lidl, *is* the contemporary assembly line. In many respects, his claim is uncontroversial. These 'concentric circles' consist of productive workers, or employees deeply immersed in the movement of commodities, then direct services workers, followed by a wider network of sales, office and retail workers at the tip of these value-producing chains.[3] Within these circles exist large-scale workplaces employing thousands of wage labourers, from hospitals and retail parks, to Amazon warehouses and care home facilities. But, as Jason Smith has asked, are these growing battalions of largely low-wage, low-skilled labourers *really* comparable to the large factories of the mid-twentieth-century Global North? What is preventing these large combines of urban proletariats from engaging in the kinds of industrial militancy which shook Britain to its core in the early 1970s?

In a service economy so dominated by William Baumol's 'cost disease', where productivity increases are marginal because the foundations of the economy are predicated on the commodification of need, this poses questions about worker power. On the one hand, while there are clear exceptions, most workers across Britain's labour market today are not necessarily pivotal to the fluid, integral connection between speed, productivity and profitability like the militant battalions of labour were in the 1968–75 wave of industrial struggle which rocked the country and brought down a Conservative government. The assembly line of so many of today's workers is acculturated to the needs of other workers, and this affects both the pace and power of workers in these vast productive chains.

On the other hand, large groups of workers across Britain's tertiary service economy find themselves situated at the end of supply chains, incapable of the kinds of disruptive, endemic power achieved by steelworkers, autoworkers and potters. The Lidl checkout worker who you purchase groceries from on the supermarket floor may bear significant associational power, but compared to the miner, their structural power is limited. They do not hold levers over a vast network of supply chains swarming in multiple geographical directions, of which they are sat at the centre, extracting and producing commodities. This doesn't mean workers are powerless. Even the Ford workers at the Dagenham plant went through two decades of organising, struggle, defeat and approximation before being able to wield the kinds of power mobilised in the late 1960s. However, their location in the production process was of incredible importance, and today the success of industrial struggle in the country's supermarkets, for example, puts a great onus on coalitions with sympathetic consumers, making the struggle over prices and wages a common one. Similarly, while teachers and nurses have considerably more leverage than the Lidl checkout worker, raising the possibility of shutting down a workplace which, by dint of dependency can disrupt wider layers of the economy, the durability of their disputes depends in part on their capacity to win support from parents and patients, a common feature of industrial action over the past decade.

This is reflected in the country's trade union figures. While trade union membership has steadily declined for the past forty years, it has dropped far lower in the private sector. Although trade unions certainly aren't the only measurement of working-class strength, it is clear that contemporary trade unionism is stronger among older cohorts of the population, namely women in the public sector and, to a lesser degree, older men in the private sector. Even though certain trade unions, such as Unite under Sharon Graham's leadership, have experienced membership rises reflective of their economic militancy in an era of inflation, the overall pattern of decline has not been reversed, with trade unions representing less than 15 per cent of the working-age population.

Another potential answer to these questions of worker power is that large portions of these workers are no longer meaningfully proletarians at all. For Marx, the concept of the proletarian implied that the workers of his day were the group of people in society without property. Drawing from the Roman juridical term 'proletarius', meaning to produce offspring, or to own no property but their own children, Marx's industrial proletariat were propertyless. Today, as this book has documented, this is not true for England's workers. Although there are still large numbers of the working class in this country who work for a wage and then go home to a distastefully expensive rental property to reproduce themselves, greater numbers could be described as formal propertarians. They may own their own home outright, they may be paying off a mortgage or they may be ensconced in a network of consumption-fuelled financialised indebtedness which accentuates the reality that they do have something else to lose other than their chains. There has been a marked decline in homeownership, from its 70 per cent peak under Tony Blair to 64.5 per cent today, as low-wage younger workers struggle to get on an expensive housing ladder, hitting the limits of constrained credit access. Unlike buying with a mortgage, which is most prominent among the top quintile of earners, or social housing, which is most popular among the lowest quintile of earners, owning outright and renting privately are both evenly diffused among all quintiles of earners, pointing not only towards the prevalence of both forms of tenure among layers of the working class, but also towards the regional distribution of class. Simply put, the bigger cities, with their property booms and expensive housing markets, are more likely to produce larger propertyless proletariats today, while the rustbelt regions have produced wider coteries of propertied workers buying cheaper houses.

The Dagenham Ford workers documented in Huw Beynon's *Working for Ford* were hesitant to embrace hire purchase debt and get on the housing ladder because of their concern that this would constrain their industrial militancy, a dilemma that has seeped into the fabric of working-class life on an ever greater scale today. Aspiring to property ownership as a source of security and comfort, alongside the disciplining effects that indebtedness has on workers' willingness to take collective action to improve their lives, *can* be a barrier to class struggle. There are, of course, exceptions. Public sector workers, from DWP supervisors to university lecturers, have been at the forefront of trade union struggles in recent years, protecting their pensions from aggressive employers and state managers. But the considerations workers weigh up, such as losing a day's wage to go on strike or risking the possibility of getting sacked, absolutely play a role in the contemporary persistence of historically low levels of industrial action. The 2023 strike wave across the public sector, privatised services and the railways, as well as among transport workers, was shaped by rising inflation *and* higher borrowing costs. The goalposts have shifted: the class politics of yesteryear have been scrambled by the individualist aspirationalism of the neoliberal period, and the expansion of financialised forms of indebtedness and property ownership create new chains binding contemporary workers to the capitalist power structure, reinforcing their dependence on it and dimming revolutionary potentialities. This challenge, when we put it into conversation with Friedrich Engels' in *The Housing Question* – castigating one father of anarchism, Pierre-Joseph Proudhon, for his openness to 'petty-propietorship' and his embrace of the petty privatisation of space and land – should provoke us to think about how the scope of possibility over work, housing and public space has been constrained by the particular ways in which the neoliberal social contract has dominated the working class.

But if we take for granted that the contemporary proletariat in this country is structurally heterogeneous, stratified across a number of different lines and complicated by its relationship to property, should we ask ourselves if it is a majoritarian social force or not? This isn't a fact we should take for granted. The industrial proletariat at the core of Marx's theory of change was the gravitational centre of a wider range of classed constellations within which it was the minority for the duration of his life. The revolutionary working class of early-twentieth-century Europe, from Tsarist Russia to Weimar Germany, was a social minority too. Adam Przeworski, arguing at the moment of social democratic impasse in the 1980s, has debated to what extent the working class is a majoritarian force at all. Across society today, according to the Office for National Statistics' breakdown of employment by occupation, around 33 million people work, three quarters of the working-age population. Thirteen per cent of those are self-employed, including disempowered proletarians in services or the platform economy, and impoverished but classically petty-bourgeois small business owners. Professional occupations and associate professional occupations, which make up roughly 17.5 million people, incorporate a range of class positions, predominantly employers, managers and supervisors, but some unsupervisory forms of labour too. Finally, there are dependants – children, the elderly and the economically inactive – constituting the non-working population, the majority of whom remain dependent on the welfare state, deferred wages in the form of pensions, or the wages of a loved one for their survival. In this sense, it can be said that the working class – not the proletariat – and its dependants constitute a formal majority of the population, but should we find this hollow statistical elaboration a comforting reworking of Marx's original theory of the revolutionary class, or a challenge to it?

One potential framing of the question of contemporary gravedigger agency has been the late Joshua Clover in his wonderful *Riot. Strike. Riot: The New Era of Uprisings*. Like Kim Moody, Clover finds himself returning to Detroit. But unlike Moody, his return is to the period of deindustrialisation and racialised obsolescence that swept across the Motor City throughout the 1970s. Sympathetic to Robert Brenner's 'long downturn' thesis and the notion that manufacturing overcapacity and competition debilitated the industrial working class, Clover argues that the weapon at the disposal of proletarians in different historical moments is conditioned by the type of capitalism which governs them. Detroit in the era of deindustrialisation was a historically unusual period for combining the strike of multiracial autoworkers with the riot of the racialised poor. Typically, however, drawing on Giovanni Arrighi's periodisations of capitalism, whereas the strike was the predominant form of struggle during productive booms, the riot has been the form most used in the pre- and postindustrial eras of capitalism. Since the 2008 financial crash, with social reproduction so thoroughly commodified, cheap goods so readily available and circulatory labour so predominant, the riot – as blockade, occupation or looting – has become the hegemonic form of struggle. The prevalence of what Clover calls the 'affirmation trap', the reality that labour ceases to be the antithesis to capital in a moment of obsolescence, is the mediating determinant behind his claim that 'riot is the modality through which surplus is lived'.[4]

This circulatory struggle, born in the food riots of the transition period between feudalism and capitalism, refined in the anticolonial revolutions of the twentieth century and filtered back into the deindustrialising West, is what Clover terms a 'counterproposal of unmanageability'.[5] With the shackling of some workers into the chains of financialisation, the exclusion of largely racialised minorities from the labour market and the state continuously attempting to deal with them carcerally as a population problem, *money prime* meets *riot prime*. In England alone, the multiracial urban uprisings of 2011, just like the reactionary pogroms of 2024, involved vast sums of people excluded from the labour market, locked out of the housing market, and subjected to significantly diminished living standards and life prospects. It is a concern of contemporary socialist horizons that the forms of social reproduction, sociality and demography so prevalent in Britain today complicate the possibilities of militant, collective organising, just as other conditions – climate crisis, sickness and stagflation – make urgent the necessity of class struggle.

Sam Wetherell, in his thrilling and rich history *Liverpool and the Unmaking of Britain*, claims that the neoliberal response to the deindustrialisation which shook Liverpudlian society can be characterised as a kind of managed obsolescence. While the Merseyside city has undergone extensive bouts of formal unemployment, conditions today differ somewhat. Instead, with unemployment sat at just beneath 7 per cent, and underemployment slightly higher, it is the nefarious category of economic inactivity, encompassing a quarter of the city's working-age population, which characterises the population beyond the wage relation. In this picture, the expansion of the gig economy has absorbed many of those previously unemployed, reconfiguring the insurrectionary worklessness of Britain's two recent multiracial riots into the competing ills of abjection and subjection, defined by the predominance of broad class insecurity and the gig economy's extraction of absolute surplus value from racialised workers, consequently weakening the standards for other workers. Joe, the ex-postal worker, reflected on Amazon's decimation of the security and structures of work in the post office, demonstrating precisely this point. But what is crucial, then, rather than simply denying that obsolescence is a cultural, political and social phenomenon, is to grasp its conjunctural specificity. The shape of obsolescence today, isn't so much managed as it is contested and disorganised, the consequence of struggles from below and assaults from above, many over the terms of disablement, as formal unemployment is vastly outnumbered by sickness, demographic ageing and labour market inactivity. These processes also produce a bifurcated proletariat, as racialised and feminised workers reproduce and serve the needs of older working-class propertarians, and an increasingly large layer of the class floats between work, welfare and the instabilities of the disorganised abandonment intertwining both. In this image of contemporary class living, the story of obsolescence told by Wetherell is recomposed under the weight of neoliberalism's own contradictions and tensions.

Tuning into the television one evening in late 2024, I was struck by an image of Fraser Nelson, former *Spectator* editor, hosting a *Channel 4: Dispatches* investigation into 'Britain's Benefits Scandal'. Speaking to multiple recipients of state disability benefits, people who had physical injuries or problems with depression, Nelson could not hide his glee when one interviewee, based in the North West of England, spoke of his inability to re-enter the labour market because of a hole in the system. Nelson, a renowned right-wing journalist, had discovered the problem with today's labour market: the country's poor are trapped in a Kafkaesque system of dependency they desperately want out of, cornered by a creaking state's failure to tilt towards workfare. Not at all interested in the stark reality that work simply does not pay anymore, Nelson gallantly asked the interviewee if he could simply go it alone and take the risk without benefits.

The interviewee, one of the millions of individuals governed by the DWP, is undoubtedly an outlier. Since the COVID-19 pandemic, 3.7 million workers in Britain have declared they have work-limiting health conditions. Much of this rise is indicative of growing mental ill health. A brief glance at the GP Patient Survey data also shows a 4 per cent increase throughout 2024 in people with a physical or mental health condition lasting 12 months or longer, and people aged sixteen to thirty-four years old are now as likely to report a work-limiting health condition as someone aged forty-five to fifty-four in the data ten years ago. These health realities and their impact on people's ability to work have been diagnosed by elites as the root cause of the nation's sluggish employment rate. A mark of the British state's inability to govern, the collection of census data on the population has broken down over the past five years. Between 2019 and 2023, the overall response rate to the Office for National Statistics' Labour Force Survey collapsed from 39 per cent to 13 per cent of invited households. But there is no doubt about the nation's problem of growing sickness. NHS waiting lists currently stand at over 7 million. Britain is part of the global tendency towards demographic ageing *but* bucks the trend in boasting of an average life expectancy shortened by two years since before the pandemic. Britain's decline as a capitalist power is mirrored by its rise as a nation of sick proletarians.

Faced with growing inactivity in the labour market, the problem of population has returned with a bang. Population, the wide-ranging matter of how we live, organise ourselves, structure society, evolve and perish, is a central question of politics, and of this book. Elites have frequently concerned themselves with its character, determined to mould ordinary people along lines that are productive and profitable. Keen to grow the national economy, shred the welfare bill and reduce immigration numbers, Keir Starmer's Labour government commits to mobilising state power to reassert the moral and disciplinary value of work among the population. These anxieties, concerned far more with their impact on employers' profits and national productivity than the health of the population, were acutely expressed by the *New Statesman*'s Andrew Marr on the progressive magazine's podcast. The famous broadcaster claimed that we now have a 'generation who haven't got the disciplines of work, haven't got the socialising that work gives you, haven't got all those things that work brings us, and if you don't get those in the first ten years, you probably will never have it'. Explicit about the need to socialise workless cohorts of the population into forms of labour exploitation, Marr is one among a growing chorus of voices interested in disentangling the nation's health crisis from its labour market dysfunction.

Alongside the state's efforts to push dozens of sick, disabled and young proletarians into the workforce by reducing benefits and scaling up state punitiveness is the perennial question confronting elites across the globe, of demographic ageing. The global dependency ratio, which measures the number of those typically in the workforce against those typically not, is also at a crossroads. Older people are living for longer, fertility rates are substantively lower and the working-age population is shrinking. According to the United Nations report *World Population Ageing 2015*, 20 per cent of the planet's population will be aged sixty or over by 2050, and one in four people will live in a country where more than 30 per cent of the population are over sixty. Furthermore, British society, reflective of large parts of the world in this instance, is simply not a place conducive to raising a child. Young adulthood in this country – faced with high rents, low wages, a collapsing graduate market and a property ladder seen by many as a distant dream – lasts a lot longer. Many continue to live with their parents into their thirties, and even if they manage to get married, buy a house and sustain a half-decent job, the average cost of full-time childcare in England is £239 per week. The claim of Marxist feminist Nancy Fraser 'that every form of capitalist society harbours a deep-seated social-reproductive "crisis tendency" or contradiction' is difficult to shy away from today.[6] The creaking neoliberal social contract, the terms of disorganised abandonment, has produced a crisis in social reproduction which has cut off for millennials and Generation Z, the attainable familial securities of older generations, just as it has stuck a roadblock right at the heart of capital's productive desires.

Now, care homes for the elderly are seen as an opportunity for financial capitalists and rentiers. Amy Horton has demonstrated that these sites of socially reproductive care have become increasingly opened up to private equity firms such as Blackstone, either through direct ownership or through the meeting of publicly paid care needs. However, this does not resolve the problem confronting a stagnant capitalist system dependent on its frictionless dynamism. The issue posed to elites is how to increase the participation and productivity of the elderly, and reduce the costs they will impose on the state through pensions and healthcare, while managing politically the reality that the elderly are the most active and influential section of the electorate. Starmer's Labour, attuned to these capitalist problems, is raising the state pension age to sixty-seven between 2026 and 2028, and reviewing a further extension later in the decade. It is also under pressure, despite commitments to the contrary, to review the triple-lock pension scheme, which commits the government to raising the state pension above whichever is highest – inflation, average wages or 2.5 per cent. Underpinning this, too, is the concern, best articulated by Charles Goodhart and Manoj Pradhan, that an ageing population may be inflationary because a shrinking working-age population lends a smaller workforce a greater degree of industrial leverage. This rubs against their own deployment of Marx's theory of the 'reserve army of labour' to explain the role that a growing pool of elderly labour plays in stifling wage growth.[7] Their original observation seems more pertinent: the growth in numbers of elderly, alongside that of sick proletarians, offers particular groups of workers, at specific chokepoints that also happen to be sites of vulnerability to contagion and disablement, an enlarged scope for wage militancy. To imagine that this isn't one concern of Labour, a party that immediately sought to wrap up the host of industrial disputes carried over from the strike wave which plagued the Tories in 2023, would be naive.

While in one breath Starmerism will persist in forcing sections of the population onto the labour market, in the other it will regulate society's most vulnerable in the interests of making us all insecure. Labour's Border Security, Asylum and Immigration Act, an evolution of Blair and Cameron's Hostile Environment, though scrapping the Rwanda scheme, maintains the Tories' migrant deportation bill and supplements it with a new Border Security Command with 'counter-terror' plans to police migrants and refugees under the rubric of combating illegal smuggling gangs. Former home secretary Yvette Cooper's early pronouncements that her department will carry out immigration blitz raids on car washes and nail bars dovetails with the government's white paper, in its aim to reduce historically high levels of immigration via a discriminatory points-based system. Accompanied by Labour's announcement that indefinite leave to remain will only be granted after twenty years and digital ID cards will be rolled out to tackle illegal immigration, this dynamic – increasingly fitted to a deeply unequal, ailing service economy characterised by demographic ageing and sicker populations that need looking after cheaply – sees a confluence between high immigration, on the one hand, and repressive border systems and revanchist discourses from above, on the other. By reinforcing forms of illegality and informality among migrant workers while dehumanising them publicly, Starmerism devastates their living conditions while reproducing conditions of precarity and competition throughout the labour market. The goal of cheap, regulated labour under conditions of hyper-exploitation – eulogised by the inflammatory comment that we are now an 'island of strangers' according to Labour's leader – coalesces with the centre's naive compulsion to triangulate on the rising nativist demands of the Farage-led Reform UK.

The truth is, from the perspective of state managers and elites, there is no easy fix – spatial, technical or otherwise – which will allow the quest for profitability to easily adjust to the problem of a shrinking working-age population. The tendency towards nativist politics and tougher immigration controls, the shrinking participation of the young in the labour market, growing disablement and sickness, and the emergent tendency towards deglobalisation, adds to the sense that we are in a stagflationary moment. Though it may help to rationalise the Bank of England's commitment to raising interest rates against the spectre of industrial militancy, whether this is a pertinent explanation of inflation's persistence, particularly with food, is another question. Economist James Meadway, refusing to accept that the climate crisis is a mere exigency to capitalism, argues that rising prices are bound up with the efforts of capitalists to offload the increased costs induced by climate change – canal droughts and dry crops – onto the population-at-large.

The instruments and institutions of economic management are undergoing a process of politicisation not seen since Thatcher's neoliberal counter-revolution. Faced with climate change, geopolitical competition and war, states have seemingly returned as agents over the sphere of life we refer to as the economy. Central banks and governments respond to inflation by raising interest rates, diagnosing the increased cost of living by reference to postwar economic orthodoxies rather than identifying the real causes. In this melting pot, human subjectivity is thrown up in the air. If you go to Lidl to buy olive oil, otherwise known as 'liquid gold', you could easily find yourself spending more than a tenner.[8] In the winter, you may end up spending a fortune on energy bills in a poorly insulated house you are now paying higher interest or rent on. It is no wonder, then, that sections of the struggling masses are shifting their own moral norms out of kilter with the establishment. The 2023 strike wave was one response which troubles Joshua Clover's claim that the riot would be the predominant form of social struggle in the twenty-first century. Even in the wake of the strike wave, the prospect of increased bills and food prices has doubled the strike rate among workers, compared with pre-2023. This doesn't represent a marked shift from the historically low levels of strike action among the population typical of the neoliberal period, but it does suggest that working-class people will use a range of different methods to meet their immediate needs.

This inflationary moment has also produced new divergences from the normative decrees of capitalist realism. Some 38 per cent of Universal Credit claimants, and six out of ten of those affected by the two-child benefit cap, are in work that does not pay enough. In this context, a new moral economy among a minority of the popular classes appears to be emerging. In his 1971 essay 'The Moral Economy of the English Crowd in the Eighteenth Century', E. P. Thompson documented the clash between trade liberalisation and price rises, and the consequential explosion of popular revulsion, food riots and theft. Today, while the crime rate in general has remained broadly static, according to the Office for National Statistics, street theft rose by 40 per cent between 2023 and 2024, shoplifting has increased by 50 per cent over the past two years and there was a 50 per cent increase in robberies of business properties last year. On one *Vice* documentary, young lads would run coordinated shoplifting operations targeting chains such as the Co-op, taking orders and requests from family and neighbours over WhatsApp voice notes, in exchange for favours in return. This, in an ongoing moral panic about the fears of an 'epidemic' in collective theft from high street stores – or 'organised looting' according to the Co-op's Director of Public Affairs.[9] On top of this, the establishment's capacity to portray benefit claimants as parasites feeding on the system-at-large confronts a softening of attitudes towards benefit fraud. The *Independent* recently reported that the proportion of people who felt it was either 'not wrong' or only 'a bit wrong' for someone claiming unemployed benefits not to report a cash income from a casual job had risen from 16 per cent to 27 per cent between 2016 and 2022. On the same note, a study from the University of Portsmouth found that the proportion of people who thought falsely claiming benefits was never justified had fallen from 85 per cent in 2011 to 67 per cent in 2023. As well as this, in response to energy regulator Ofgem threatening to lift the energy price cap in 2022, 200,000 people committed to a campaign of non-payment, with pollsters estimating 3 million would refuse payment of energy bills were Liz Truss not to reduce the cap. The old elite categorisations of productive and parasitic are hitting their limits in the face of the crisis.

We must see these shifting moral economies and forms of dissent, illegality and survivalism in the context of a politically and socially disaggregated working-class subjectivity, lacking the lifeworlds, cultures, institutions and power that defined large quarters of proletarian life throughout the twentieth century. We live in an age of what sociologist Émile Durkheim described as 'anomie' – a profoundly alienated state of affairs whereby both meaning and connection are difficult to come by. As early as 2014, an Office for National Statistics report depicted Britain as the loneliest society in Europe. In 2018, following the recommendations of the Jo Cox Commission on Loneliness, Theresa May created a Minister for Loneliness portfolio in government. Six years later, though, the *Lonely Nation* report found that a significant majority of the population felt lonely, left out, isolated and lacking in companionship, with many respondents attributing this breakdown to the absence of family or marriage, the rise of individualism, and the dearth of opportunities to meet people and forge common bonds. Working-class life today is characterised better by its individuation than its collectivism. To speak of the *breaking* of the working class in this country is no mere exaggeration. The defeats imposed on us throughout the late twentieth century and into present times, are not, I believe, irreversible. But they are profound. Without holding up the world before 1979 as a utopian paradigm, physically, socially, organisationally and culturally, the working class has been treated to a rupture that has fundamentally changed its character in the interests of its class enemies. *We* have been devastated. Changing that, grasping the space between the increasing far-right influence over our communities and the necessity of what Paul Gilroy has described as the 'unkempt, unruly, and unplanned multiculture', one must ask what kinds of coalitions and cultures could facilitate the entrance of emancipatory agents into the sphere of British politics.[10]

To put it bluntly, the force most successfully pulling portions of the working class towards it, animating the despairing, revanchist impulse that underscores the competitive impoverishment of life in this country today, is Farage's Reform UK. On course to win the next general election, it is at the gravitational centre of an orbiting far-right ecology, taking advantage of an amenable media environment, largely owned by billionaire racists; an influencer cadre from Andrew Tate to Tommy Robinson, telling young men in particular that their problems lie with feminism, the 'wokerati' and 'military age' refugees; an insurgent fascist street movement which, unsatisfied with its instigation of pogroms in 2024, continues to protest outside hotels housing asylum seekers, falsely claiming that these warehouses are luxury resorts for sexually predatory men; and a Labour government that tries to outdo its far-right rivals by vindicating Reform UK's message at every opportunity it gets. If there is a political force in this country prepared to take advantage of the possible dissolution of the two major parties, it is this one.

Farage's story is simple too. This country is in decline because it has allowed too many foreigners to storm its gates, let families shrivel, let the workshy and the criminal residuum get away with murder, and put up with the elite class putting down our nation.

The threat of Reform UK is not just down to the charisma of its incredibly effective leader. Nor is it simply the acceptance of its story in conditions of deep-seated abandonment, isolation and racialised labour market competition. It is also down to, in a way that Boris Johnson in 2019 could not even dream of, its capacity to put its tanks on Labour's lawn, claiming to want to ignite reindustrialisation, give tax breaks to those who have children and give the political class a bloody nose. And it is working. Reform UK is not just succeeding in hoovering up the traditional Conservative vote among the wealthier quarters of the country in the English South, it is dominating in precisely the kinds of places that I have tried to centre in this book. It is projected to win majorities in all seats across Stoke-on-Trent, as well as dominating the municipal elections in 2027. To make matters worse, I have encountered credible reports from organisers across the country that Reform UK branches are even beginning to step onto what should be the radical left's terrain: organising nappy banks and targeting people at bus stops where routes have been cancelled in areas poorly serviced by transport networks. Faragism is further disassembling the possibility of a collective class subject, and creating an insurgent coalition centred on nationalist grievance and revanchism, by speaking to the multiple ways people feel abandoned. That the young are developing hardening attitudes on crime and welfare, contrary to the moral economy permeating since the mid-2010s, is an acute example of how Farage is forcing almost all his political rivals to accede to his own narrative by occupying the centre ground of British politics.

Those of us who desire a world predicated on living dignified, free lives should ask ourselves what it would mean to assemble a coalition capable of overturning the politics and culture of Faragism *as well as* transcending capitalism. At one level, the third condition underlying Marx's theory of the revolutionary class – the collective consciousness of working-class life – has often been at risk of being taken for granted by the left. Mike Davis, in his seminal *Old Gods, New Enigmas: Marx's Lost Theory*, illuminates in great detail the ways in which radicals, socialists and communists at the start of the twentieth century consciously took advantage of the collectivising animus of capitalism's social form, in the workplace or the slum neighbourhood, and organised workers and their dependants to fight for better wages, community infrastructure, social reforms, international solidarity and, ultimately, revolution. But Marx's theory wasn't necessarily consistent or automatic, either. Workers in heavy industry, such as miners and engineers, were among the most powerful cohorts of the revolutionary alliances which shook Europe after the First World War, but they did not necessarily constitute the natural social base of communism in Europe's newborn capitalist democracies. Similarly, Marx's evasion of largely female domestic labourers, the biggest fraction of proletarians throughout his lifetime even if not the most powerful, signals that we may need a more expansive notion of the classed coalitions that occupy socialist attention today.

As this book has demonstrated, national declinism over the past forty years has thrived on the idea that there are sections of the population – migrants, refugees, Muslims, the unemployed, the disabled and the criminalised – who are portrayed as exterior to the national community. This narrative thrives precisely because it focuses, laser-eyed, on the large coteries of the populace who have been excluded from the political economy of neoliberalism. Across towns and cities, reactionary political actors hold up the asylum seeker who has moved into the local hotel, the person with substance abuse problems who takes shelter in the derelict house on your estate and the disabled worker on benefits as totemic symbols of the decline which has held the country back. Instead of the elites who have ravaged our living conditions, the landlord who sits on dilapidated brownfield land until they can be sure they are going to make an easy fortune or the employers who work us hard and devastate our bodies, we are constantly told that the most vulnerable people in our society are the ones who are denying us a future.

We need stories and alliances that can begin to reverse this account of our misery. Contrary to the Marx of the late 1840s, who saw in society's destitute and marginalised the 'lumpen proletarian' raw materials of the European counter-revolutions, we must build a version of socialist majoritarianism which refuses the elevation of the productive over the unproductive, the formal over the informal or the independent over the dependent. The working class, disaggregated across the space of British capitalism's uneven economic geography, consists of homeowners, renters, underemployed, unemployed, the disabled, informal proletarians, workers in the field of production, social reproduction and circulation, people treated as vagrants, and the incarcerated and excluded. Phil Burton-Cartledge, drawing on Maurizio Lazzarato, argues that the 'immaterial labour' of today's political economy – commodified affective and cognitive capacities – embeds a sociality among a multicultural workforce. And while this is true to some extent, the overarching story in this book implies that we cannot take this for granted.[11] Horizons have shrunk, and our people are poorer, sicker and lonelier than they have been for some time.

The crisis in British capitalism's ability to reproduce itself and its subjects has created a greater need for forms of interdependency, repair and care among our people. Against the suspicious paranoia of Faragism, we need a socialist politics which reclaims human beings made surplus to capital's requirements as an integral component of our coalitions. Only by confronting head-on the racialised and classed portrayal of crisis so pervasive within British culture, through stories and organising experiences of popular community, decarcerality and empowerment, can we begin to rearticulate the declinist reading of national entropy as one of abandonment. There is a version of Marx which can assist us with this project. In perhaps his most provisional work, the *Grundrisse*, written in the late 1850s, the German revolutionary takes great joy in mocking the moral outrage of West Indian plantation owners, avowedly vexed that the free black people of Jamaica had taken to producing 'only what is strictly necessary for their own consumption', valuing 'loafing (indulgence and idleness) as the real luxury good'.[12] This was in contrast to the slaver's obsession with fixed capital, profitable natural resources and working the population's fingers to the bone. This version of Marx, putting a primacy on the free time of formerly enslaved labourers, which finds echoes in *Capital*, when he argues that the 'realm of freedom' can only be realised when the 'realm of necessity' is fulfilled and the working day shortened, strikes right at the heart of the kinds of politics which must underscore contemporary socialist majoritarianism. Against Nigel Farage's appeals to 'alarm clock Britain', we must assert the moral supremacy of the lie-in. Counter to the idea that we must work hard for thirty-seven hours per week, from our late teenage years until our late sixties, the new socialist coalition must struggle for greater control over our time, our lives, our homes and the physical spaces of our neighbourhoods, towns and cities. We need a vision of the future which encompasses all segments of the popular classes – including those deemed alien or illicit – under the banner of freedom, interdependency and care.

Marx's thesis that the working class is a gravedigger is, as China Miéville has noted in his reading of 'The Communist Manifesto', a metaphorical wager, rousing the proletarians of his day into action.[13] Today, if we want to recover the pulse of socialism, its heartbeat, perhaps the working class is simultaneously nurse, cook *and* gravedigger. Repair a battered working class which has been abandoned, and as so often happens, abandoned itself in the process; feed a working-class population the food, culture and collectivity it is so often denied by high prices and privatised space; and create the conditions in which a diverse, stratified class can free itself by digging the grave of capitalism for good. Only then, can the nurse, cook and gravedigger become obsolete roles, replaced simply by liberated human beings, with a range of skills and talents, living full, disalienated lives.

Conclusion: Good Life Syndrome

We come from ruins, but we are not ruined.

'Modernism in the Streets', Marshall Berman

'There are, in fact, no masses; there are only ways of seeing people as masses. In an urban industrial society, there are many opportunities for such ways of seeing,' argued Raymond Williams in 1958, observing how capitalist rule projected images of people through culture, the economy and society, in ways that coalesced with attempts to manage populations profitably.[1] Politics today is full of such efforts. The 'Red Wall', the 'left behind', 'Mondeo Man', 'Whitby Woman', all constitute attempts to produce the kind of people elites actually want to claim some governing legitimacy over. These signifiers rationalise complicated human beings with contradictory ideas into static blocs imagined by pollsters and pundits, and mobilised by politicians to serve concrete ends, in a moment when politics could not be more distant from people.

This book's intention has been to trouble elite stereotypes, separate what is superficially true about these caricatures from what is inevitably false, consider what their articulation tells us about our society today, and provide an alternative way of thinking about working-class life historically and in the present. The task has been to take the changing forms of population management dominant across the twentieth and twenty-first centuries and, returning to Williams once again, 'consider, personally and collectively, what these have done to our thinking'.[2]

An insight driving this book has been the claim that the neoliberal social contract and its subsequent breakdown have produced a crisis of class subject formation. It's not that there hasn't been popular resistance. Avoiding the tendency to peripheralise working-class people, I have tried to make clear that each transformation in the methods of capitalist control and exploitation has been met with a wave of mass revolt. For the five years that I have lived in Stoke-on-Trent, I have witnessed first-hand Black Lives Matter protests, a Palestine solidarity movement involving thousands at its height, strikes by rail workers and posties, the building of community infrastructure meeting people's food and clothing needs, the wonderful combination of art, ecological and social justice spearheaded by the Portland Inn Project and others in the city, and hundreds of people from all backgrounds mobilising to defend their communities from street fascism. None of this is to be sneered at. In fact, in many ways, this activity is the raw material of radical transformation. But, the disconnect from all these struggles to a mass, emancipatory politics that can transform society and halt the range of overlapping catastrophes affecting our society demonstrates the necessity of a felt, totemic and powerful movement for socialism.

I moved to a place seemingly unlike where I grew up, and saw in Stoke-on-Trent everything I loved about London before it was transformed by gentrification. It is different, do not get me wrong. The experience of infrastructure if you're in Stoke, is completely different compared with that of a Londoner, and for the worse. People in Stoke are more likely to own homes and drive. People in London earn far more but the cost of living is a fortune. Both are denied access to arts and culture, but in Stoke because the cultural offer is restrained, and in London because lots of people simply cannot afford it. But, in moving to this new place, and seeing a deep commonality with the postindustrial, multicultural London I grew up in, it struck me that both places face attempts by elites to construct an image of them quite foreign from the one they live on an everyday basis. One of the tasks of this book has been to develop a different picture of the complex ways in which class oppression is felt and lived – namely through the lens of *organised* and *disorganised* abandonment – taking seriously the idea that working-class people, both in the country's large metropolises and the rustbelt regions, have an inordinate amount in common, despite the best efforts of the political class to portray otherwise. Ultimately, when one considers which places decide elections and how crucial areas like Stoke-on-Trent have been to the left's misfortunes, most notably in 2019, this book has been driven by a sense that the people of both the rustbelt regions and the cities deserve better, and their ability to realise this is bound up with their potential to make common cause. The terrifying alternative to that possibility is further decomposition and recrimination, opening the way for forces such as Farage's Reform UK to win in places like the Potteries, and so win nationally.

Underscoring the problems of building coalitions between different forms of working-class protagonism is a concomitant crisis of futurity. When I walk from Stoke-on-Trent station to Hanley Park, I see the island in the park's lake, which carries a series of large metallic word sculptures. Hanging by a thread, letters out of joint, some floating in the lake, the sculptures read, 'I see you standing there as if on a distant horizon, I reach out and our hands touch.' The decay of the physical environment in Stoke, a reminder that little changes for the better, reinforces the notion that a transformational horizon feels increasingly distant. The experience of class *breaking* documented in this book speaks to an assault that was waged on emancipatory agents, their bodies, their lifeworlds, their moral norms and their sense of political possibility. Imagining a positive sense of what the future might hold for us requires birthing anew the cultural, social and political sinews which could bind new class subjects together with insurgent, emancipatory visions, across different experiences of space and time.

To develop a notion of socialist freedom fit for today's world, we must immerse ourselves in our communities, talking to neighbours about the issues which confront us and organising alongside one another to change those objects of oppression, domination and everyday abandonment which drive our people into the hands of the far right. This call to live among the people speaks to the necessity of experimentation. Stuart Hall, in 1983, remonstrated with the orthodox left: not only can we not afford a calcified image of the perpetually recomposing masses, we also cannot take our ideas for granted. We must recognise the fortitude of a 'Marxism without guarantees', and act accordingly. Social transformation in the interests of the working-class majority is not inevitable, and today it is not controversial to say it is unlikely.

The unfolding nexus of disorganised abandonment, reiterated as declinism by contemporary elites, is felt by working-class people as it is expressed in the notes passed among the files and folders of General Practitioners: 'Shit Life Syndrome'. Against this, we need to disseminate a practicable rendition of the Good Life Syndrome. When society today offers us abjection at work, we must struggle for a fruitful, non-exploitative relationship to work which prioritises democratic control and reduced working time. When politicians pathologise us and tell us we are unhealthy because we eat shit food, take drugs and doss in squalor, we must fight for a right to food, health, housing, leisure and welfare. And when we are offered the 'antisocial century' by platform capitalists reconfiguring our brains through the smartphone, we must organise for social spaces and real human connection instead.

Ruth Wilson Gilmore, a figure who has left an indelible stamp on this book, articulates abolitionist politics – seeking to rid society of carceralism, capitalism and domination – as the resurrection of 'life-affirming institutions' against the oppression of organised abandonment. Today, in the face of *disorganised* abandonment, we require a do-it-yourself socialism which seeks to combine the construction of popular institutions aimed at defending, repairing and empowering the people through tenants' unions, worker organising, community kitchens, popular psychiatry, health clinics and political parties, with a majoritarian politics of transformation geared towards challenging the state and creating new forms of life, love and sovereignty.

Insisting that these two poles be bridged is dependent on the notion, essential in the fight against national declinism and capitalism, that our movements should be mass, and that no one should be left behind by the socialist project. Historian Barnaby Raine, in his seminal PhD thesis 'Immanent Freedom', examines debates within the socialist movement – first between reformists and revolutionaries, then between social-democratic and communist figures, and then between Stuart Hall and Ambalavaner Sivanandan. He locates a historical tension within the coalitions of the left between a socialist majoritarianism inflected by its electoral inclinations and desire to conquer the nation state, and a militant minoritarianism which focuses on rupture, mass action from below, internationalism and genuine universalism. The socialist and communist movements of the early twentieth century sought to connect their ultimate goal of a free, classless planet with struggles over reforms in the present, first through the united front and then, particularly during the experience of the German revolution, in the form of a workers' government against capitalism. André Gorz, the ecological Marxisant who advocated for a postindustrial socialism, argued that the left should turn to 'non-reformist reforms', enacting policy demands which could bake into the political and social fabric an irredeemable turn towards decommodification. Underlying these rubrics of transformation is the idea that we must confront the capitalist system in its totality, while marshalling that opposition into a real, liveable movement that is translatable to millions, felt by them and fought by them as well.

As Rose Hunter, an exemplary image of the radical individuals produced by the twentieth century, remarked to me, 'I'm not academic, but I think capitalism's in serious fucking downfall at the minute.' Rose is right, and to avoid capitalism pulling us all down with it, we need a project which can seek out today's nurses, cooks and gravediggers, forge common cultures and identities, and build a new world worth living in. We need to organise for popular power ourselves, because nobody is coming to save us.

Acknowledgements

Attempting to write a book while working and being involved in successive waves of mass organising is not advisable. In the end, I finished it in no small part thanks to the help, sustenance and advice of an intellectual, activist and friendship community far bigger than just me. First of all, this book would not have even been an idea without the wonderful Rosie Warren taking a punt on me and making it happen. I am incredibly grateful for your encouragement and editorial genius.

The generation of ideas represented in this book are the result of a number of collectives, institutions and campaigns which provided forums for debate, education, divergence and experience. Thank you to revolutionary socialism in the twenty-first century, Salvage, Left on Read, Frightful Hobgoblins, Drop City Books, Historical Materialism and Organising 4 Popular Power.

To Max, Doris, Habibi and Ramona: it would be an overestimation to suggest that any of you helped me with the book, but your love, klutziness and walks have made this whole experience a tad lighter.

Families can be a complex thing for many, but I've been blessed with grandparents. Granddad, Gran and Billy, the three of you in very different ways made the childhood of a pretty-weird kid just a bit easier.

Importantly, this book is the result of a thousand conversations, heartfelt moments, organising experiences and reflections among friends and comrades who I am incredibly grateful for: Josh, Samir, Aydin, Matt, Neil, Sai, Vallu, Charlotte, Raymond, Seb, Joe, Riya, Shereen, Shamma, Callum, Brendan, China and Satnam – you've all been legends.

To my friends in Stoke: Ruth, Liam, Alice, Rebecca, Cal, Chloe, Paul, Louise, Mark, Fran, Alex, Daryl, Joe, Rose and Waqas. Thanks for making me feel that your city is my home, teaching me so much about the struggles and greatness of its people in the process. I do not know of a place in the world that feels like a warm cuddle as much as this one.

There are people without whose help the completion of this book would have been impossible. Jaice and Harry: thanks for being constant sources of support and sound-boarding. It is in our conversations that the ideas in this book have been developed and sharpened, as well as moments of great relief found. Aamna and Shanice: when we began building a decades-long friendship, who would have thought we would all end up writing books? Well, me actually – to a lifetime of cackling, troublemaking and thinking together. Tomos, thanks for poring over drafts, debating the particulars with me and being an all-round great friend. It does not go unappreciated. Barnaby, it's a source of great happiness for me that we share such a deep-seated partnership. This project has your mischievous fingerprints all over it, and our books are, for better or for worse, two sides of the same coin we both seek to abolish. Jonny, I simply would not be the person I am today without our friendship, and this book is littered with over a decade of collective problems, anxieties and debates that we've had to work out the hard way. I hope you see your imprint in its character, even where you disagree. Ingrid, throughout it all, having you as my best friend in this journey called life has been a privilege. Leaving London was a difficult thing to do, but your enduring love and light made it unregrettable. You have so often been my north star, even when we have both been lost.

Notes

Preface

1 Ruth Wilson Gilmore, *Abolition Geography: Essays towards liberation*, London: Verso Books, 2022, p. 196.
2 Raymond Williams, *The Long Revolution*, Cardigan: Parthian, 2013, p. 68.

1. Marx in the Potteries

1 Otto Saumarez Smith, *Boom Cities: Architect-planners and the politics of radical urban renewal in 1960s Britain*, Oxford: Oxford University Press, 2019, p. 168.
2 Ibid., p. 168.
3 Karl Marx, *Capital: A Critique of Political Economy, Volume 1*, England: Penguin Books, 1990. pp. 354–6.
4 Ibid., p. 378.
5 J. B. Priestley, *English Journeys*, London: HarperNorth, 2023, p. 442.
6 Ibid Priestley p. 445.
7 Dominic Davies, *The Broken Promise of Infrastructure*, London: Lawrence & Wishart, 2023, p. 11.
8 Sacha Hilhorst, 'A Tale of Two Towns: Economic Disadvantage and Political Disempowerment in Ex-Industrial England', common-wealth.org, 22 November 2024.
9 Richard Castle, 'Controversial Poll Ranks Stoke-on-Trent among "Worst Places to Live in UK"', *Sentinel*, 7 February 2023.
10 William Wallis, 'Financial "Jaws of Doom" Threaten English Councils as Cost Pressures Mount', *Financial Times*, 17 July 2023.

11 Sacha Hilhorst, 'A Tale of Two Towns: Economic Disadvantage and Political Disempowerment in Ex-Industrial England', common-wealth.org, 22 November 2024.
12 Ibid.
13 Quoted in Kim Moody, *On New Terrain: How Capital Is Reshaping the Battleground of Class War*, Chicago: Haymarket Books, 2017, p. 83.
14 Jessica Murray, '"We Can't Go Back": Staffordshire Firms Fight to Keep Ceramics Tradition Alive', *Guardian*, 18 February 2025.
15 Gabriel Winant, *The Next Shift: The Fall of Industry and the Rise of Healthcare in Rustbelt America*, Cambridge, MA: Harvard University Press, 2021.
16 Sam Wetherell, *Liverpool and the Unmaking of Britain*. London: Head of Zeus, 2025, p. 15.
17 Jon Burnett, 'The New Geographies of Racism: Stoke-on-Trent'. London: Institute of Race Relations, 2011, p. 4.
18 Neil Smith, 'Gentrification and the Rent Gap', *Annals of the Association of American Geographers*, 77(3), 1987: 462–5 at 545.
19 Phil A. Neel, *Hinterlands: America's New Landscape of Class and Conflict*, London: Reaktion Books, 2018, p. 97.
20 Brett Christophers, 'Revisiting the Urbanization of Capital', *Annals of the Association of American Geographers*, 101, 2011: 1347–64.
21 David Harvey, quoted in Christophers, 'Revisiting the Urbanization of Capital', p. 1350.
22 Henri Lefebvre, *The Urban Revolution*, Minneapolis, MN: University of Minneapolis Press, 2003, p. 15.
23 Henri Lefebvre, *The Production of Space*, Oxford: Blackwells Publishing, 1991, p. 282.
24 David Harvey, 'The Urban Process under Capitalism: A Framework for Analysis', *International Journal of Urban and Regional Research*, 2(1–3), 1978: 101–31, at 120.
25 Jon Burnett, 'Geographies of Racism: Stoke-on-Trent', *Institute of Race Relations*, 2001, at irr.org.uk
26 Rob Moore, 'Nigel Farage on Britain's SHOCKING Decline and Becoming the Next Prime Minister', *YouTube* (2025).
27 Serena Barker-Singh, 'Something Remarkable Is Happening with Gen-Z' – Is Reform UK Winning the "Bro Vote"?', *Sky News* (2024).
28 Alberto Toscano, *Late Fascism: Race, Capitalism and the Politics of Crisis*, London: Verso Books, 2022, p. 33.
29 J. B. Priestley, *English Journeys* [e-book], London: Harper Collins Publishers, 2023, p. 400.

2. Disorganised Abandonment

1 George Osborne, 'Chancellor's Speech on Changes to the Tax and Benefit System', gov.uk, 2 April 2013.

2 Adrienne Roberts, 'Household Debt and the Financialization of Social Reproduction: Theorizing the UK Housing and Hunger Crises', *Research in Political Economy*, 31, 2016: 135–64, at 4.

3 Maya Goodfellow, *Hostile Environment: How Immigrants Became Scapegoats*, London: Verso Books, 2019, pp. 2–3.

4 David Cameron, 'PM's Speech on the Fightback after the Riots', gov.uk, 15 August 2011.

5 Chris Grover, 'Violent Proletarianisation: Social Murder, the Reserve Army of Labour and Social Security "austerity" in Britain', *Critical Social Policy*, 39(3), 2018: 335–55, at 11.

6 Peter Mair, *Ruling the Void: The Hollowing of Western Democracy*, London: Verso Books, 2013, p. 254.

7 Tom Hazeldine, 'Revolt of the Rustbelt', *New Left Review*, 105, 2017: 51–79, at 65.

8 Sarah O'Connor, 'Left Behind: can anyone save the towns the UK economy forgot?', *Financial* Times, 15 November 2017, ft.com.

9 Mark Fisher, *Capitalist Realism: Is There No Alternative?*, London: Zero Books, 2009, p. 21.

10 Satnam Virdee, *Racism, Class and the Racialised Outsider*, London: Bloomsbury Academic, 2014, p. 3.

11 Ash Sarkar, *Minority Rule: Adventures in the Culture War*, London: Bloomsbury Publishing, 2025, p. 274.

12 W. E. B. Du Bois, *Black Reconstruction in America: Toward a History of the Part Which Black Folk Played in the Attempt to Reconstruct Democracy in America, 1860–1880*, Milton Park: Taylor & Francis, 2017, p. 46.

13 Antonio Gramsci, *Prison Notebooks: Volume 1*, New York: Columbia University Press, 2011, p. 641.

14 For more on 'mental sediments', see Rosa Luxemburg, 'The Mass Strike' (1906), marxists.org.

15 Satnam Virdee and Brendan McGeever, 'Racism, Crisis, Brexit', *Ethnic and Racial Studies*, 41(10), 2018: 1802–19, at 1809.

16 E. P. Thompson, *The Making of the English Working Class*, London: Pantheon Books, 1964, p. 9.

17 'John McDonnell Says Grenfell Fire Was Social Murder', bbc.co.uk, 16 July 2017; Ashley Cowburn, 'Grenfell Tower Fire: Jeremy Corbyn Suggests Using Empty Kensington Properties for Victims', independent.co.uk, 16 June 2017.

18 Quoted in Owen Jones, *This Land: The Struggle for the Left*, London: Penguin Books, 2020.

19 Quoted in Gabriel Pogrund and Patrick Maguire, *Left Out: The Inside Story of Labour Under Corbyn*, London: Random House, 2020, p. 152.

20 Leo Panitch and Colin Leys, *Searching for Socialism: The Project of the Labour New Left from Benn to Corbyn*, London: Verso, 2020, p. 244.

21 Karl Marx, *Capital: A Critique of Political Economy, Volume 1*, England: Penguin Books, 1990, p. 362.

22 Phil Burton-Cartledge, *The Party's Over: The Rise and Fall of the Conservatives from Thatcher to Sunak*, London: Verso Books, 2023.

23 Duncan Thomas, 'The Long Conservative Decline', revsoc21.uk, 21 November 2019.

24 James Scott, *Seeing Like a State: How Certain Schemes to Improve the Human Condition Have Failed*, London: Yale University Press, 2020.

3. The Personal Society

1 Antonio Negri, *Revolution Retrieved: Writings on Marx, Keynes, Capitalist Crisis and New Social Subjects (1967–1983)*, London: Red Notes, 1988, p. 12.

2 John H. Goldthorpe, David Lockwood, Frank Bechhofer and Jennifer Platt, *The Affluent Worker: Industrial Attitudes and Behaviour*, Cambridge: Cambridge University Press, 1968, p. 28.

3 Ibid., p. 87.

4 John Westergaard, 'The Rediscovery of the Cash Nexus', *Socialist Register*, 7, 1970: 120.

5 Stuart Hall, 'A Sense of Classlessness', in *Selected Political Writings: The Great Moving Right Show and Other Essays*, edited by Sally Davison, David Featherstone, Michael Rustin and Bill Schwarz. Durham, NC: Duke University Press, 2017, pp. 28–46, at p. 39.

6 Peter Malpass, 'Fifty Years of British Housing Policy: Leaving or Leading the Welfare State?', *International Journal of Housing Policy*, 4(2) (2004): 209–27, 216

7 Selina Todd, *The People: The Rise and Fall of the Working Class*, London: John Murray, 2015, pp. 184–5.

8 '1959 Labour Party Election Manifesto', labour-party.org.uk, 2001.

9 Huw Benyon, *Working for Ford*, England: Penguin Education, 1979, p. 122.

10 Guy Ortolano, 'Begrudging Neoliberalism: Housing the Fate of the Property-Owning Social Democracy', in *The Neoliberal Age? Britain since the 1970s*, edited by Aled Davies, Ben Jackson and Florence Sutcliffe-Braithwaite, London: University College of London Press: 2021, pp. 319–35, at p. 319.

11 Stuart Hall, 'Supply of Demand', in *Selected Political Writings*, pp. 47–69, at p. 59.

12 Otto Saumarez Smith, *Boom Cities: Architect Planners and the Politics of Radical Urban Renewal in 1960s Britain*, Oxford: Oxford University Press, 2020, pp. 15–16.

13 Guy Ortolano, *Thatcher's Progress: From Social Democracy to Market Liberalism through an English New Town*, Cambridge: Cambridge University Press, 2019, p. 227.

14 Christopher Harvie, *Fool's Gold: The Story of North Sea Oil*, London: Penguin Books, 1995, p. 47.

15 Raymond Williams, *The Long Revolution*, London: Parthian Books, 2013, p. 342.

16 Stuart Hall, Chas Critcher, Tony Jefferson, John Clarke and Brian Roberts, *Policing the Crisis: Mugging, the State and Law and Order*, London: Red Globe Press, 2019, p. 245.

17 Alastair Bonnet, 'How the British Working Class Became White: The Symbolic (Re)formation of Racialized Capitalism', *Sociology Lens*, 3(3), 1998: 316–40, at 330.

18 Enoch Powell, 'Enoch Powell's "Rivers of Blood" Speech', anth1001.wordpress .com, 2014.

19 Tom Nairn, *The Break-Up of Britain*, London: Verso Books, 1981, p. 276.

20 Annie Phizacklea and Robert Miles, *Labour and Racism*, London: Routledge & Kegan Paul, 1980, p. 169.

21 Guy Ortolano, *Thatcher's Progress: From Social Democracy to Market Liberalism through an English New Town*, Cambridge: Cambridge University Press, 2019, p. 411.

22 Keith Joseph, 'Speech at Edgbaston ("Our Human Stock Is Threatened")' margaretthatcher.org (1974).

23 Nicholas Ridley and Nationalised Industries Policy Group, 'Ridley Plan', otjc. org.uk, 15 March 2024 (1977).

24 Simon Joyce, 'Why Are There So Few Strikes?', isj.org.uk, 5 January 2015.

25 Arthur McIvor, *Working Lives: Work in Britain since 1945*, London: Palgrave Macmillan, 2013, p. 232.

26 Beatrix Campbell, *Wigan Pier Revisited: Poverty and Politics in the 80s*, London: Virago Press Limited, 1985, p. 176.

27 Quoted in Huw Beynon, 'The Politics of the Collapse in Britain Manufacturing', *Critique: Journal of Socialist Theory*, 16(1), 2007: 1–22, at 7.

28 Huw Beynon, 'The Politics of the Collapse in Britain Manufacturing', *Critique: Journal of Socialist Theory*, 16(1), 2007: 1–22, at 11.

29 Diarmaid Kelliher, *Making Cultures of Solidarity: London and the Miners' Strike*, Abingdon: Routledge, 2021, p. 106.

30 Jim Tomlinson, 'The Failures of Neoliberalism in Britain since the 1970s: The Limits on "Market Forces" in a Deindustrialising Economy and a "New Speenhamland"', in *The Neoliberal Age? Britain since the 1970s*, edited by Aled Davies, Ben Jackson and Florence Sutcliffe-Braithwaite, London: UCL Press, 2021, pp. 94–112, at p. 84.

31 Linda McDowell, *Redundant Masculinities? Employment Change and White Working Class Youth*, Oxford: Blackwell Publishing, 2003, p. 56.

32 Beatrix Campbell, *Wigan Pier Revisited: Poverty and Politics in the 80s,* London: Virago, 1984, p. 189.

33 Ibid., p. 190.

34 Noel Whiteside, *Bad Times: Unemployment in British Social and Political History*, London: Faber and Faber Limited, 1991, p. 6.

35 Simon Peplow, *Race and Riots in Thatcher's Britain*, Manchester: Manchester University Press, 2019, p. 102.

36 Darcus Howe, 'Babylon and the Bobby: Brixton before the Uprising', in *Here to Stay, Here to Fight: A Race Today Anthology*, edited by Paul Field, Robin Bunce, Leila Hassan and Margaret Peacock, London: Pluto Press, 2019, p. 57.

37 Quoted in McIvor, *Working Lives: Work in Britain since 1945*, London: Palgrave Macmillan, 2013, p. 231.

38 Paul Gilroy, 'The End of Anti-Racism', *Journal of Ethnic and Migration Studies*, 17, 1990: 71–83, at 207.

39 Ambalavaner Sivanandan, *Communities of Resistance: Writings on Black Struggles for Socialism*, London: Verso Books, 2012, p. 212.

40 Paul Gilroy, 'The End of Anti-Racism', *Journal of Ethnic and Migration Studies*, 17, 1990: 71–83, at 207.

41 Paul Gilroy, *There Ain't No Black in the Union Jack: The Cultural Politics of Race and Nation*, Abingdon: Routledge, 1992, p. 189.

42 Kieran Connell (2019), *Black Handsworth: Race in 1980s Britain*, Oakland, CA: University of California Press, p. 90.

43 Neil Brenner, *New States Spaces: Urban Governance and the Rescaling of Statehood*, Oxford: Oxford University Press, 2004.

44 Diane Frost and Peter North, *Militant Liverpool: A City on the Edge*, Liverpool: Liverpool University Press, 2013, pp. 17–18.

45 David Harvey, 'From Managerialism to Entrepeneurialism: The Transformation in Urban Governance in Late Capitalism', *Geografiska Annaler: Series B*, 7, 1989: 3–17, at 11.

46 Nicholas Deakin and John Edwards, *The Enterprise Culture and the Inner City*, New York: Routledge, 1993, pp. 99–102.

47 London, The Bishopsgate Institute Archive, Widgery/14 (Accessed 12 June 2023).

48 Finn Gleeson, 'Stories from London's Docklands: Heritage Encounters, Deindustrialization, and the End of Empire', *Journal of British Studies*, 61(5), 2022: 970–95, at 973.

49 Ibid., p. 984.

50 Jack Copley, *Governing Financialization: The Tangled Politics of Financial Liberalization in Britain*, Oxford: Oxford University Press, 2021, p. 121.

51 Leila Simona Talani, *Globalization, Hegemony and the Future of the City of London*, Basingstoke: Palgrave Macmillan, 2012, p. 63.

52 Stuart Hall, 'The Great Moving Right Show', in *Selected Political Writings*, p. 181.

53 Alexander Gallas, *The Thatcherite Offensive: A Neo-Poulantzian Analysis*, London: Brill, 2006, p. 221.

54 Simon J. Charlesworth, *A Phenomenology of Working-Class Experience*, Cambridge: Cambridge University Press, 2000, p. 71.

55 Ibid., p. 196.

56 Huw Beynon and Ray Hudson, *The Shadow of the Mine: Coal and the End of Industrial Britain*, London: Verso Books, 2021, pp. 252–3.

57 Margaret Thatcher, 'Interview for *Sunday Times*', margaretthatcher.org (1981).

4. The Long '90s Were Really Long

1 Stuart Hall, 'Parties on the Verge of a Nervous Breakdown', *Soundings*, 1 Autumn 1995: 19–34, at 19.

2 David Harvey, *The Condition of Postmodernity*, Oxford: Blackwell Publishing, 1990, pp. 186–7.

3 Arthur McIvor, *Working Lives: Work in Britain since 1945*, London: Palgrave MacMillan, 2013, p. 195.

4 Helen Charman, *Mother State: A Political History of Motherhood*, London: Allen Lane, 2024, p. 263.

5 Quoted in Selina Todd, *The People: The Rise and Fall of the Working Class*, London: John Murray, 2015, p. 339.

6 John Welshman, *From Transmitted Deprivation to Social Exclusion: Policing, Poverty and Parenting*, Bristol: Bristol University Press, 2007, p. 214.

7 Ibid., p. 216.

8 Colin Crouch, 'Privatised Keynesianism: An Unacknowledged Policy Regime', *British Journal of Politics and International Relations*, 11(3), 2009: 382–99, at 392.

9 Matthew Watson, 'House Price Keynesianism and the Contradictions of the Modern Investor Subject' in *Housing Studies*, 25(3), 2010: 413–26, at 417.
10 Ibid., p. 420.
11 Owen Hatherley, *A Guide to the New Ruins of Great Britain*, London: Verso, 2011, p. xix.
12 Andrew McCulloch, 'Localism and Its Neoliberal Application: A Case Study of West Gate New Deal for Communities in Newcastle upon Tyne, UK', *Capital and Class*, 28(2), 2004: 133–65.
13 Stuart Hall, 'The Multicultural Question', in *Race and Difference*, edited by David Morley, Durham, NC: Duke University Press, 2021, pp. 403–4.
14 Richard Power Sayeed, *1997: The Future That Never Happened*, London: Zed Books, 2017, p. 44.
15 Nadine El-Enany, *(B)ordering Britain: Law, Race and Empire*, Manchester University Press: 2020, p. 135.
16 Colin Webster, 'Race, Space and Fear: Imagined Geographies of Racism, Crime, Violence and Disorder in Northern England', in *Capital and Class*, 27(2), 2003: 95–122, at 96.
17 Ted Cantle, 'Community Cohesion: Report of the Independent Review Team', tedcantle.co.uk (2001).
18 Mike Makin-Waite, *On Burnley Road: Class, Race and Politics in a Northern English Town*, Chadwell Heath: Lawrence & Wishart, 2021, pp. 170–1.
19 Ted Cantle, 'Community Cohesion: A Report of the Independent Review Team', tedcantle.co.uk (2001).
20 Alana Lentin and Gavan Titley, *The Crises of Multiculturalism: Racism in a Neoliberal Age*, London: Zed Books, 2011, p. 38.
21 Bridget Anderson, *Us and Them? The Dangerous Politics of Immigration Control*, Oxford: Oxford University Press, 2013, p. 56.
22 David McNally, *Global Slump: The Economics and Politics of Global Resistance*, Binghampton, NY: PM Press, 2011, p. 4.

5. Whither Gravediggers?

1 Karl Marx, 'Karl Marx to Ludwig Kugelmann, 17 March 1868', marxists.org.
2 Anwar M. Shaikh and E. Ahmet Tonak, *Measuring the Wealth of Nations: The Political Economy of National Accounts*, Cambridge: Cambridge University Press, 1994, p. 29.
3 Kim Moody, *On New Terrain: How Capital Is Reshaping the Battleground of Class War*, Chicago: Haymarket Books, 2017.

4 Joshua Clover, *Riot. Strike. Riot: The New Era of Uprisings*, London: Verso Books, 2016, p. 288.
5 Ibid., p. 272.
6 Nancy Fraser, 'Contradictions of Capital and Care', *New Left Review*, 100, 2016: 99–117, at 100.
7 Charles Goodhart and Manoj Pradhan, *The Great Demographic Reversal: Ageing Societies, Waning Inequality, and an Inflation Revival*, London: Palgrave Macmillan, 2020, p. 125.
8 'Price of Olive Oil Up 50% in One Year', *eurostat*, 27 February 2024.
9 Emine Sinmaz, '"It's Organised Looting": UK in Grip of a Shoplifting Epidemic, Say Store Owners', *Guardian*, 15 September 2023.
10 Paul Gilroy, *After Empire: Melancholia or Convival Culture?*, Oxfordshire: Routledge, 2005, p. x.
11 Phil Burton-Cartledge, *The Party's Over: The Rise and Fall of the Conservatives from Thatcher to Sunak*, London: Verso Books, 2023.
12 Karl Marx, *Grundrisse: Foundations of the Critique of Political Economy*, London: Penguin Classics, 1973, pp. 325–6.
13 China Mieville, *A Spectre, Haunting: On 'The Communist Manifesto'*, London: Head of Zeus, 2021.

Conclusion

1 Raymond Williams, *Culture and Society: Coleridge to Orwell*, London: Hogarth Press, 2017, p. 814.
2 Ibid.